FIRST STAGE

A DRAMA HANDBOOK FOR SCHOOLS AND YOUTH THEATRES

FIRST STAGE

A DRAMA HANDBOOK
FOR SCHOOLS
AND YOUTH THEATRES

Ginny Graham

Northcote House

British Library Cataloguing-in-Publication

A catalogue record of this book is
available from the British Library

ISBN 0 7463 0643 1

© Ginny Graham 1993

First Published in 1993 by Northcote House Publishers Ltd,
Plymbridge House, Estover, Plymouth PL6 7PZ, United Kingdom.
Tel: (0752) 735251; Fax: (0752) 695699

Typeset by PDQ Typesetting, Stoke-on-Trent
Printed and bound in Great Britain by BPCC Wheatons Ltd, Exeter

Contents

To past members of
North Powys Youth Theatre,
and present members of
Montgomeryshire Youth Theatre,
with thanks for all the fun.

Ginny Graham

Introduction

Drama work with young people is one of the most exciting and challenging creative activities which a teacher or group leader can experience. A well-motivated group, working in harmony on a common purpose, provides opportunities for its members' self-development and enhancement of their artistic and social awareness. The leader plays an essential part in this process, helping to establish and maintain the ethos of the group, its working practices, and the accepted norms of behaviour.

It is mainly through the activities which take place in workshop sessions that the group ethos is established, and self-awareness and empathy develop during the process of acquiring and practising skills and exploring ideas through the medium of drama. The organisation and running of workshops is therefore of central importance in the work of an adult who takes on the responsibility of leading a group. The work is demanding, but the rewards are great. Young people, particularly in their teenage years, are challenging, unpredictable, and at times quite baffling. They are also warm, funny, sensitive and hardworking. To share their experiences in creative work, and to be part of the process of their development into maturity, is energising and fulfilling.

Drama has always been something of a Cinderella subject in schools. There was a period in the late 1960s and through the 1970s when advances in thinking about its educational role were translated into sound practice. The academic and also the business world began to acknowledge the importance of drama in the development of the individual. New examinations were devised, validated, and became part of the established curriculum. But over the past decade the emphasis in education has switched to a more pragmatic programme. Science, business studies and fact-based learning are judged a more suitable preparation for adult life than the more creative and imaginative subjects.

Drama does not (at the time of writing) stand as a subject in its own right within the national curriculum. Nevertheless, it is still widely taught in schools, across the age range, and in a great many establishments to examination level, both GCSE and Advanced.

Many colleges run performance arts-based courses. In the early years of secondary school, cross-curricula arts courses are operated, with drama as a component equal to other subjects. Despite the odds against it, drama still seems to be maintaining its place in the educational arena.

The new methods of drama teaching mentioned earlier placed the focus on the experience of the individual; the positive personal development which could be brought about through physical self-expression and exploration of issues relevant to the participants. Some of the language and techniques of theatre were borrowed for use in the service of education. This approach could provide valuable experience under the direction of a well-trained and confident teacher.

Unfortunately, few schools gave drama a high enough priority to fully equip themselves with the relevant staff to provide this experience for all pupils, though there was a noticeable increase in the provision of drama studios and theatre hardware. In current practice, drama lessons are frequently organised by the English department, and often given to the least experienced staff as part of their initiation into the role of teacher. Lacking understanding of either the philosophy or the method, these teachers are ill-equipped to cope with the practical or the developmental aspects of the subject. A few have an intuitive feeling for what they should do, and in effect teach themselves how to 'teach' drama. Many more, with their classes, endure rather than enjoy the shared experience. In such cases, drama sessions can be frustrating, aimless and sterile for the participants, and disheartening, if not frightening, for the teacher. A school hall, or a drama studio, full of energetic youngsters and none of the foci which provide built-in control in the classroom—tables, chairs, teacher's desk, blackboard—can provide an environment which could have been specifically designed for educational disaster.

But it does not have to be disastrous. Given the right approach, with firm strategies and clear objectives, drama sessions can be the high point of the timetable for students and teacher. Drama is the one subject in which the concepts of 'getting it right' or 'giving the wrong answer' should never intrude. The only way anyone can be 'wrong' is if what is done is negative or damages what someone else does. With that proviso drama sessions provide a unique opportunity for students and teacher to work together in a way in which the ideas, skills and innate creativity of each member of the group can be explored and expressed. Once the parameters of the working environment have been established by a sympathetic teacher, confident in his or her methods and aims, the group feels secure in its work, and free to express itself individually and collectively, exploring and creating, accepting the ideas of others, working constructively within a shared experience.

Those classes which are lucky enough to be taught by a teacher who (with or without formal training) has a belief in and enthusiasm for this work derive great benefit from an activity which is very different from all their other school experiences. They are given the opportunity to re-create and express in physical terms both real and imagined worlds. Frequently this work, of intrinsic value, provides a foundation for further experiences, in which they take on the disciplines and skills necessary for performance, moving from the rather private world of the drama lesson to the public world of theatre.

At a time when drama in schools has been enjoying rather mixed fortunes, the last decade has seen an unprecedented growth in the youth theatre movement, within the UK and throughout the world. Youth theatre is a self-chosen activity, and it places great demands on those who participate in it. Youth theatre has its social aspect, of course, but this is subservient to the commitment to the highly concentrated and demanding work which takes place in most youth theatre workshop sessions, and certainly when a production is under way.

Throughout the country, new youth theatre groups are being established in towns and rural communities. The backing organisations are very varied. Some youth theatres are set up as part of the outreach community programme of regional theatre companies, some under the auspices of local authority youth services. Some amateur theatre groups, particularly in rural areas, organise youth sections working under the wing of the adult group. And some are set up as totally independent organisations, run by the members themselves, with or without an adult leader. Youth club leaders are also facing demands for drama workshops, and leading them themselves or, if possible, bringing in specialist workers for this purpose.

In all these cases, group leaders come from a variety of backgrounds, with differing levels of experience in the specialist skills required to carry out the work effectively. Some have been trained for either education or the theatre — sometimes both. But (as with the non-specialist teacher faced with a drama class in school) many have the enthusiasm, enjoy working with young people, but have no training in the skills and strategies required to carry through such work in a way which produces an enjoyable and satisfying experience for all concerned. When this happens the group's members become disaffected, numbers diminish, the remainder spend more time making coffee and chatting than engaging in any constructive activity, and eventually the group folds. Thus all the creative potential is lost, and the members and their leader are left with perhaps some pleasant memories, but also a sense of waste and regret.

But this need not happen. As in the school situation, the potential benefits of well-organised, positive and enthusiastic youth theatre work are enormous, contributing in a very special way to the group and individual development of the young people involved, and to the social and cultural life of their community.

What is the relationship, then, between school drama and youth theatre? Do they need to be seen as discrete activities? How wide is the common ground which they share? I have worked for many years with young people in schools and youth theatre groups, and I believe there need be no fundamental difference in the approach to the work, and its content, wherever it is carried out.

The reasons why young people choose to join a youth theatre are probably as diverse as the individuals concerned. Undoubtedly, some see it as the first stage in a theatrical career. The majority, however, value it for its own sake. It gives them something which no other organised youth activity seems to offer.

What is this? I was once asked to lead a workshop as part of a youth theatre festival under the title 'The Power of Youth Theatre'. In order to try out some ideas in advance, I asked members of the youth theatre which I lead to produce an acrostic on the word 'power' as it applied to youth theatre. These are some of the results.

People	Performance	Pow!
Often	Of	Oooh!
Willingly	Words	Waah!
Exert themselves	Elaborates	Everything's
Regularly	Reality	'Riggling

These examples of an immediate response to the request to analyse something which is at the same time abstract and familiar to those who gave these answers seem to encapsulate the nature of youth theatre – the unforced commitment, the special experience, and the sheer fun. If the kind of work which is undertaken in youth theatre sessions provokes this reponse, would not a similiar methodology benefit similar work in schools?

I believe that drama work in schools can fail because the young people involved are not given the tools to do the job. They are expected to work cooperatively without learning to trust each other. They are expected to improvise without any preparation in the necessary techniques. They are expected to play in role without learning how to create another character. Youth theatre workers use methods which enable young people to develop and apply these skills.

Just as methods and styles develop and change in the theatre, so they can in youth drama. Currently, much of the most exciting work which is being developed by theatre companies is based on the physical aspects of performance. Without diminishing the importance of words, the language of the body is becoming central in the dramatic exploration and presentation of material. This aspect of the evolving language of theatre is one which young people find particularly exciting. Their energy and inventiveness can be positively applied to alternative methods of self-expression, in which they can be given freedom to experiment and extend their range of communication and interaction. Through awareness of movements in the profession from which many of their working practices are taken, youth drama leaders, in or outside schools, can offer new approaches to their groups. As theatre is continually experimenting and evolving, so can youth drama work.

Youth theatre took the best from the advances in educational drama, and combines this with the skills and disciplines of the theatre. In the same way, education can benefit from the work which has been done in the more informal environment of youth theatre. A good drama lesson can be indistinguishable from a good youth theatre workshop. The atmosphere is relaxed, but purposeful. The participants are self-disciplined, the teacher's status is that of *primus inter pares* rather than authoritarian. The nature of the work in hand–improvisation, devising, the acquisition and practice of skills – can be identical. Equally, each can be as bad as the other. A drama lesson in which pupils are told yet again, without guidance or preparation, to 'do something on bullying – or soap operas – or conflict with parents' has its parallel in youth theatre sessions dedicated to improvisations in which the dreary repetition of simulated sexual activity, violence and expletives is varied only by the sterile re-creation of television advertisements.

In the best work, wherever it takes place, sessions have been planned and structured as part of an ongoing process. The overall aim is to enable young people to explore their own ideas and experiences, and the world in which they live, using the techniques and language of theatre. These they need to learn, and it is the acquisition and practice of skills, alongside the dramatised expression of their own ideas, or the exploration of relevant works by established writers, that is fundamental to good working practice.

What is the particular nature of youth theatre and drama work, and what are the benefits to participants?

The innate creativity of every human being is widely accepted during the early years, in the home with caring parents, in playgroup and primary school activities. Children are encouraged to paint, make models, dress up and act out fantasy games. The stimuli which feed their imaginations are an integral part of the process of education. But as they grow older and enter adolescence, these stimuli and opportunities for imaginative creation are gradually withdrawn. It is easier for everyone if they learn to conform and accept rather than question and create.

There are, of course, exceptions; individuals whose creative urge, in whatever discipline, remains strong and develops into adult life and who become the artists and discoverers of their generation. But the creative powers are slow to die in most individuals, and in adolescents they are lying dormant, and can be reanimated given the right circumstances and environment. Drama work gives just such an opportunity, and the satisfaction which both groups and individuals experience when they work together to make something new through their own powers of expression can become a factor which informs positively their transition to adult life.

As I said earlier, in drama work the only way in which anyone can be 'wrong' is by harming another person's work. The atmosphere of acceptance and appreciation of each individual and what he or she has to offer builds self-confidence, particularly in the quieter, more reticent members of the group. At the same time, the brashness of the more extrovert and domineering members is modified, as they learn that this is an activity in which a more sensitive and thoughtful attitude is most valued.

The coming together of many different personalities when engaged on a mutually agreed task, whether a game, exercise, short improvisation or full-scale production, builds a group identity and sense of trust and interdependence among the members. There is no sense of competition. Each person is valued for his particular skills and contribution to the group's activities. A well-established and harmonious group is generous in its appreciation of each person's worth, and has a strength and confidence which enables it to welcome and assimilate new members, who will quickly respond and adapt to the ethos of the group.

Young people are, in general, extremists. They see things in absolute terms, right or wrong, black or white, fair or unfair. This is also how they tend to express their ideas, and they can be right. But sensitive drama work can enable them to explore such issues across the continuum between extremes, to develop an empathic awareness of the viewpoints of others. Thus their own ideas can become better informed and balanced. A fourteen-year-old girl, taking on the role of her mother waiting up late to hear her come home from a party, can explore the emotions which she can only guess at from the reaction which she has experienced. This is, perhaps, a mundane example, but it represents one aspect of the value of such work.

Of equal importance is the opportunity to explore and dramatise larger issues of justice and injustice which they see in the world around them, and which they often feel powerless to influence. The grand themes of politics and human behaviour impinge forceably on the lives of the young: we expect them to grow into adults who can deal with them, but we frequently neglect to allow them the opportunities for exploration and debate which will enable them to understand the world which others have made for them to live in, and empower them to be active in bringing about positive change.

Young people deserve a forum in which to present their viewpoints: the theatre can give them this. And it is just as much 'theatre' when taking place in a school hall as on stage in a fully equipped theatre building. In well-run workshop sessions, they can acquire the necessary skills to present to an audience, whether of their peers or adults, their concerns, their philosophy. They can present with objectivity, by taking on other roles. The theatre has always had the function of confronting humanity with itself, and when this is done with the freshness and energy which young people bring to it, it is doubly effective.

Such work allows them to expand their horizons. It enables them to move beyond their own experience of the world. In improvisation, they can inhabit different personae, different societies, different environments. When texts are used, as part of the workshop process or for performance, they are brought into contact with a great range of viewpoints and presentations of life. The language and thoughts of the best writers from the past and the present can become familiar, as they use them in the way in which those writers intended, for dramatic presentation of the human condition. No sterile analysis of a text can give a young person so much insight to its meaning and impact as can its use in the stimulating and supportive environment of a drama workshop.

All of this lies behind my opening statement that drama work with young people is one of the most exciting and challenging creative activities which a teacher or group leader can experience. Is the picture of a well-motivated, mutually supportive, creative group over-idealistic? To those who have endured rowdy classes in school halls, or watched the junior section of an amateur theatre group limp through yet another ill-directed production of *Oliver*, it may seem so. But in schools, colleges and youth theatres throughout the country sound, relevant and well-organised work is taking place, and the methods of achieving this are not secret.

I have often been told by teachers, youth club leaders and adult amateur drama group members 'we want to run drama workshops, but we don't know how to do it'. The willingness is there, but the knowledge and expertise is lacking. As in so many other activities, success is founded on simple practicalities. 'What do I do with them?' You work with them. Such work has a variety of components, a selection of which can be brought together to achieve your obectives.

The first part of this book deals with three fundamental areas – preliminary work, improvisation and character work. Models of games and exercises are provided, linked by discussion of approaches and strategies. Using this material, it should be possible to construct individual workshop sessions, and courses of varying lengths, to be used with groups of young people aged from approximately twelve upwards. With modification, most of it is quite suitable for younger age groups. I have used it for them myself. How the material is put together is very much a matter of individual needs and choice. The resource section at the end of the book gives a couple of suggested models, one for a single workshop session, one for a four-session course.

The second part of the book deals with performance, both of devised work and scripted plays, suggesting approaches to preparation and rehearsal which integrates the production into the workshop process. Back-up material can, again, be found in the resource section.

Like a recipe book, this is designed for practical use – for the kitchen, not the coffee table. There is no magic potion which will ensure instant success in youth drama work. Everything depends on the choice and blending of the individual ingredients – the people, the methods, the material. Much of the excitement comes from experiment, from taking risks, learning from mistakes, celebrating and building on success. Experienced workers may well find familiar material here, but, hopefully, may also find some fresh ideas and approaches. Those new to the work can be reassured that it has all been tested in many differing circumstances and has, on a number of occasions, produced rewarding results.

Please note that the pronoun 'he' and its derivatives have been used throughout the text to avoid pedantic clumsiness.

Chapter 1
Preliminary work

The work to be described here is preliminary in two ways. When a newly-formed group begins to work together it is necessary to establish the working methods and create the atmosphere which will be conducive to productive and enjoyable sessions. The members of the group may already know each other, but for drama purposes they will need to get to know each other in a different way. If the group is a voluntary one, outside school, many of them will be strangers to each other, and to you, and you will need to establish working relationships, both between the members of the group, and between you and them.

If the emphasis in these early sessions is on games and simple skills exercises there is the opportunity for each person to participate and contribute immediately, without feeling a pressure to perform or to expose any personal uncertainties. A good working atmosphere can thus be established quickly.

The work is also preliminary in that warm-ups, games and exercises are useful at the start of every session, however long the group has been working together. They re-establish the group dynamic and identity, shifting the focus of each individual from what he or she has been doing prior to the session to the work in hand. Any newcomers can be assimilated quickly through the shared enjoyment of physical activity.

These preliminary games and exercises are designed to focus the group's attention on the self-control which is essential if useful work is to be done. They build up concentration, give opportunities for non-aggressive physical contact, and help to confirm a sense of equality and the confidence of each member of the group.

In early sessions with a new group, approximately half the time available can be usefully allocated to this kind of work, and in later stages about a quarter. Even when there are demands on your time, such as during the final stages of rehearsal for performance, a short session of preliminary work can pay dividends in establishing concentration and self-control.

The selection of games and exercises described here come under general headings of physical and walking warm-ups, introductions, trust exercises, voice exercises, concentration and observation, ensemble and group work, and energy-releasing games. The activities chosen for any session, and the order in which you use them, will depend on the needs of the group and the session which you are running.

Physical warm-ups

Before starting on any kind of work which demands movement, it is a good idea to hold a short session of controlled exercises to relax and warm the muscles. Even young bodies get stiff joints, and some insurance against accidental physical strain or injury can be taken out by making sure that bodies are supple at the start of the session.

There are many exercises and techniques which can be used. If you have any experience of yoga, tai chi or dance it is quite possible to put together a sound warm-up routine based on the early stages of such disciplines. The purpose is to make sure that all the major joints of the body are gently exercised, and that a sense of physical awareness and response to the needs of their bodies is instilled in the members of the group. These exercises should start gently, and can then become more vigorous.

A simple routine is set out below. As in many of the exercises, the group should stand in a circle. You will need to talk them through the stages, demonstrating, observing, helping and correcting as the exercise progresses.

1.   Stand in a balanced posture, feet slightly apart, weight evenly distributed, arms and hands relaxed at sides. The head should be balanced at the top of the neck. Imagine there is a cord fixed to the crown of your head, attached to the ceiling directly above you. Bounce gently on the balls of your feet as if you are suspended from the string – like a puppet. This position is the point of balance, to which you return at the end of each section of the exercise.

2.   We now isolate and work each part of the body in turn. First, massage the muscles at the back of the neck, then roll the head round slowly, letting it drop under its own weight, first onto the chest, then round to the left, then back, then to the

right. Repeat this four times to the left, then four times to the right. Don't do this fast, because that can make you dizzy.

3. Roll the left shoulder backwards four times, then forwards. Do the same with the right. Then both together. Feel the stretch across the back between the shoulder blades, and in the chest muscles. Next swing the whole of the arm round, first backwards, then forwards, left and right separately, then together.

4. Stretch the arms up to the ceiling, stretching the fingers up as far as they will go, pushing up with the top of the head at the same time. Feel the pull on the muscles in the spine and the back of the legs. The heels should not leave the ground. Let the hands drop from the wrists, forearms from the elbows, then the whole arms from the shoulders to the sides.

5. Hold out the hands and rotate them gently from the wrists. Flex and stretch the fingers quickly twenty times. Relax and shake arms and hands gently.

6. Place the feet slightly wider apart, place the hands on hips, and stretch from the waist, first to the left then to the right. Next, roll the top half of the body round in a circle, keeping legs and hips firm, first in one direction, then the other.

7. Flex the knees slightly, and roll the hips in a circle, left then right. (This usually provokes giggles, lewd comments, and breaks down any remaining inhibitions.)

8. Come back to the point of balance. Standing on the right leg, raise the left with the knee flexed, turn the foot from the ankle, first one way and then the other. Then swing the lower leg in a circle from the knee, and then the whole leg from the hip. Repeat with the other leg. You need to make sure there is plenty of space for this.

9. Standing upright at the point of balance, feet about eighteen inches apart, let the body relax down, starting with the head, ending with flexed knees, over a count of eight. Hang there, relaxed, for a count of eight, then come up slowly on a count of eight, ending with the head.

10. Shake out hands, arms, feet, legs, and return to the point of balance.

This is a very simple, basic sequence of warm-up movements, which can be extended and adapted, slowed down or made more vigorous as needed. It works best if you do it with the group at the same time as talking them through. This can be tricky at times, because you need to see what they are doing, but it is possible with some ingenuity. It is important that the exercises are taken seriously, even the ones that provoke giggles, and you should help them by demonstration and by checking their body posture.

A more vigorous alternative is to tell them that they have a piece of chewing gum in their mouths, which is first chewed until soft, then spat out onto the right hand, then transferred to the left, and they are trying to shake it off. The gum is then transferred to different parts of the body, and each part is shaken to 'remove' it. This is a more chaotic warm-up, as well as being faster, and can be a useful ice-breaker exercise for a reserved group, but is not recommended for a group you want to quieten down.

It is not always necessary to have the kind of concentrated physical warm-up described above. It really depends on the nature of the work you are going to do. It does, however, have the advantage of establishing control and concentration, and warming up the muscles for more demanding physical work. You may, however, want to go straight in with other exercises, which involve physical movement of a more informal kind.

Walking warm-ups

These are some simple and non-threatening routines for new groups, and good revision work for established ones. They can be adapted, extended and used in a number of ways. Again, you need to talk them through.

1. (a) On your own, walk round the room at a moderate pace. Do not follow anyone, or walk alongside anyone. Don't make eye contact or physical contact with anyone. Look for a space and walk into it, always turning on a curve. Cover the whole area of the room.

   (b) Without walking in a straight line, cross the centre line of the room on each journey. Make no contact with anyone else. Be aware of the space around you, above you, the feeling of the floor under your feet, your relationships to the other bodies in the room.

(c) Keep walking, and choose another person to keep in your sight as you walk, but do not walk beside or follow him or her.

(d) Still keeping in visual contact with the first person, choose another whom you want to keep away from. Keep walking until the command 'freeze'. (The 'freeze' command is a useful one which can be used at any time. Establish it early as a control mechanism.)

2.   (a) Walk as in 1 (a) (above).

(b) While you are walking, point to and call out the name of all the objects in the room – wall, ceiling, chair and so on.

(c) Now stagger the point and the name. If you look at the wall first then point at the ceiling and shout 'wall', look at the chair and shout 'ceiling' and so on.

(d) Walk round and touch all the objects in the room. Experience the different textures, warmth or coldness, hardness or softness.

(e) On 'freeze' sit down in a circle and share impressions of the room, each person giving one word or a short phrase which describes the objects or the atmosphere in the room.

3.   (a) Start walking, at first making no eye contact.

(b) As you walk, make firm eye contact with everyone you meet. Try to make this contact with everyone in the room. Then change back to making no eye contact.

(c) Stop walking. The group is divided into As and Bs. Begin walking again. The As hold firm eye contact with everyone they meet, and the Bs drop their glances as soon as contact is made. Change over.

(d) On 'freeze' sit in a circle and discuss the different feelings and atmosphere which this exercise produces.

4.   (a) Start walking.

(b) On the command, stand as close as possible to someone wearing (for example) red, blue, green; someone with long hair; someone with blue eyes.

(c) On the command, everyone who had cornflakes for breakfast run to a point in the room; everyone who watched breakfast television; everyone who travelled by bus – and so on.

These routines help to establish concentration, controlled movement, and an atmosphere for group work. Some are rowdier than others, and can therefore be used to enliven and relax a group which is quiet or tense.

Introductions

It is important that everyone knows each other's name at an early stage, and introduction games should be used whenever new members join the group. They also help to establish concentration. As with many other exercises, the circle is the best working shape.

1.   (a) A bean-bag (easier to catch and less potentially damaging than a ball) is thrown around and across the circle, and each person who catches it calls out his name.

(b) Now throw the bean-bag and call out the name of the person it is thrown to. Make sure no one is left out.

2.   (a) One person calls out his name, points to another person in the circle, and moves to his space: that person does the same until everyone in the circle has moved. The movement should be continuous, each person setting off as he is pointed to.

(b) The first person calls the name of the one he is going to change with, the second does the same, and so on.

3.   One person says a name and what he likes, beginning with the same letter 'I'm Belinda and I like boys'. The person beside her introduces her to the one on the other side. 'This is Belinda and she likes boys' and then adds his or her name and liking, and so on round the circle, the list increasing all the time.

4.   The first person calls his or her name and makes an extravagant body shape or gesture. The whole group repeats the name and gesture, and so on round the circle.

At the end of an introduction game in a circle, you can instruct everyone to change places, then choose one person to put everyone back in their original places, using their names. Choose an alert and confident person to do this, otherwise it can take a long time and become boring.

A more leisurely and developed introduction exercise is as follows:-

5.   Put the group in pairs, preferably pairing people who do not know each other. Give them time to talk together with the instruction to find out three distinct things about their partners. When they have done so, each person introduces his partner to the group and tells what he has found out.

Trust

Trust is one of the most important things to establish between the members of a group at an early stage. As they continue to work together, they will find themselves in situations in which they need to know that they can rely on each other without reservation. They need to overcome physical repressions, to be able to touch, hold and support each other. Young people can be extremely timid and self-conscious about physical contact, and not only in mixed groups. The kind of aggressive (if playful) physical contact of the sports field or the playground is something they understand, even though some may not enjoy it. However, controlled, supportive physical contact is very different from such casual encounters, and needs to be learned and practised.

Trust games and exercises help to overcome the psychological resistance to physical contact, when a disciplined structure is provided in which inhibitions can be discarded as personal responsibility for the well-being of others is accepted. This kind of activity is important throughout all the work the group undertakes, and it is usually very popular.

Some exercises do require care in matching sizes and relative weights of the pairs or groups which are carrying them out, so be sure that an eleven-stone boy is not to be supported by his eight-stone girlfriend.

The Physical Knot
If you do have an inhibited group, this is a good ice-breaker, as it is a fairly boisterous whole-group activity.

The group holds hands in a circle. Break the circle at one point, and instruct the two people at the ends to re-form the group into a knot by leading it, both ends at once, towards the mid-point, stepping over and crawling under the joined hands. At no time must anyone let go of the hands he is holding. Once the group is throughly tangled, instruct the two leaders to unscramble it, still without shifting the original hand-clasps, and to re-form the original circle.

Running Blind
This is another vigorous group trust exercise. There are several alternative versions. These are two of them.

The group divides and stands at two sides of the room, facing each other. One person is blindfolded (or can be trusted to keep his or her eyes shut) and is led to one of the unoccupied walls. He or she is instructed to run straight towards the wall opposite without slowing down, and to stop when his or her name is called. It is the responsibility of the group to stop him or her before he reaches the wall, but as close to it as possible.

Members of the group take it in turn to be catchers. Two people physically stop the runner before he or she collides with the wall. As confidence increases, the runner can be instructed to keep going at full speed until he or she is halted by the linked hands of the catchers. They should make contact at stomach level, and the runner should be told to tense his stomach muscles at the moment he makes contact.

Every member of the group should take a turn at running, though with a large group this may be too time-consuming. If anyone really does not want to commit himself to these, or any other of the trust exercises, you need to deal with the reluctance gently, but try to persuade him to take part over time.

The activities described above are vigorous and not particularly subtle, though they do demand concentration and self-control. The following exercises are more tightly disciplined. The first three are for pairs, the others for larger groups. When any pair work is undertaken, it is important that each part of the activity is done by each of the pair.

Music can be an aid to concentration for some of these exercises, played quite softly in the background. Choose fairly anonymous tapes, so that they concentrate on the activity rather than the music.

Sticking

Physical contact is by the touching index fingers of the right hands. The contact is light, and there should be no pressure exerted by either. One person closes his eyes and maintains the contact as his partner moves the hand through different planes. Make sure that they do not hook their fingers together. This is something of an exercise in empathy. It can be developed by one person leading the other around the room, with only this minimal contact, eyes closed. You can set out a series of obstacles, such as chairs, but it is usually sufficient with a large group that they simply avoid each other. The basic instruction is that there should be no collision or physical contact with another pair, or anything else in the room, and the exercise should be done without talking.

Different touches

One of the pair closes his eyes and stands still, while the other touches him on arms, legs, head and body with a variety of light touches–with the whole hand, with one finger, with a light stroke. Alternatives are to hold the hand close to the body without touching, just close enough for there to be an exchange of body heat, or to blow gently on the skin. The touches should be random in timing and position and, again, the exercise must be done silently. This exercise can be done in threes, with two people touching the third.

Talking through maze

This is rather more noisy, and you do not need music in the background. It can be done by two or three pairs at a time. Set up a maze of obstacles, and blindfold one of each pair. Their partners have to talk them through the maze from one end of the room to the other and back to the start, using only the commands 'go', 'stop', 'left', 'right', 'forward', 'back', 'down', 'up', and 'turn'. The aim is to avoid any contact with the obstacles. A lot of concentration is needed by the blindfolded player in order to hear only his partner's voice, and to block out all other sounds.

Tense and relax
This is done in threes. One sits on a chair, the other two, standing at each side, apply pressure with their hands to different parts of his body – shoulders, forehead, thighs, calf muscles and so on – while he pushes that part of the body back against the pressure. As the pressure is applied the verbal instruction 'tense' is given by the others, and as it is released 'relax'. The pressure should be held for approximately five seconds.

Swaying
This requires groups of five or six. One stands in the middle of the circle formed by the others. Initially, the group should be quite close together; with experience it can be spread wider. The person in the middle stands relaxed and balanced, feet slightly apart, eyes closed. The others stand well-balanced, with one foot in front of the other, ready to accept the weight of the person in the middle smoothly and confidently. He sways (or is gently pushed) forwards and is caught, and then his body is passed across and around the circle. He should never have to move his feet unless there is some uncertainty about being caught confidently. Those supporting must always be ready to take the weight of the body and pass it on smoothly.

This is not an easy exercise to get right in the early stages. Initially, there will be some giggling, staggering and falls. You need to emphasise that the person in the middle – and everyone will have a turn – should have a good experience and have no fear of falling. Lots of concentration and self-discipline are needed to make this experience enjoyable, and it can be very enjoyable. Make sure, before you start, that the members of each group are well matched for height and weight, and be prepared to step in and help out.

It is worth persevering with. Like all the other exercises, once a group has understood how to do it well, it can pass on the necessary skills to newcomers, and this kind of induction of new members, and the confidence and concentration of the group as a whole, is the springboard for all other activities.

Pendulum

A variant on the above, for the more experienced. Three stand in a
line, and the one in the middle is pushed (as in *swaying*) between
the two, always with a relaxed yet upright body and feet firm on
the ground. As they become more confident and trust grows, this
exercise can be carried out over a surprisingly wide space and at
great speed.

Run, fall and recover

A whole-group exercise, and a very simple one. The group runs at
random around the room, and individuals fall to the ground at will.
They are immediately helped to their feet by those who happen to
be closest to them. This is one of the simplest exercises, in which the
individual does not have to think to choose, but acts as a part of the
group by carrying out the instruction.

The final exercises in this section are always popular, because of
their apparent danger. In fact, as long as everyone concentrates,
there is minimal risk.

Horizontal lifts

Divide the group into two. The people in each half then lift and
carry each member of the other half from one end of the room to
the other, the body being horizontal. Show them how to lift the
body (which should be relaxed) cleanly and evenly, working in
pairs. Each body should be placed carefully on its feet at the end of
the journey. You will find that they soon find it more enjoyable and
easier to carry the bodies at arms' length above their heads.

Fall and catch

Six or eight people stand in two lines, close together, facing each other.
They make a safety net with their hands, *not* by clasping hands or
wrists, but by placing the hands, palm upwards, staggered so that the
palm of the first hand in the line is alongside the wrist of the person
opposite, and so on down the line. Rings and watches should be
removed. The instruction is to concentrate on the faller and give with
the weight of the body, placing it firmly on its feet after the fall. The
faller stands at a height at the end of the line, preferably on a steady
block. His feet should not be lower than the catchers' hands. At an
agreed signal, he lets himself drop horizontally onto the safety net of

the catchers' hands. This can be done facing forwards or backwards, though backwards is best.

Some people do not enjoy falling, and should not be pressured into doing this exercise. Except in the case of the most experienced groups it should never be done unsupervised. However, the weight of the faller seldom proves a problem as it is evenly distributed. I have seen an eleven-stone man 'caught' by a group of ten and eleven-year-old children, working under supervision.

Voice Exercises

Confident use of the voice is very important in drama work. At a later stage, if you are preparing for a public performance, it will be necessary to help them to learn how to project their voices through space, and where to pitch their voices in different environments. It is necessary, however, that they should be able to use their voices confidently in workshop situations. The most interesting improvisations can be marred by mumbling.

Vocal warm-ups need to be part of the regular pattern of warm-up exercises. As with the physical warm-ups, the muscles used should be exercised gently to avoid strain. Generally, the work is done by the group together as a whole unit. The following routine can be adapted and used as necessary.

1. Each person massages his own face, concentrating on the jaw and throat muscles.

2. Squeeze the face together tightly, then stretch it as wide as possible, then relax.

3. Open the mouth wide, stick out the tongue and try to use it to touch the nose and the chin alternately.

4. Waggle the tongue loosely around the mouth.

5. Run through a series of repeated consonantal sounds, grouping them together in sound patterns. Explain the difference in the use of the lips, tongue and the jaw position when making similar sounds such as *t* and *d*, *p* and *b*, *s* and *z*.

6. Control the breathing, breathing in over a count of four, then

out, increasing the count to six, eight, ten. Vocalise a sustained vowel sound over an out-breath, gradually increasing and decreasing the volume, and extending the length.

7.   Run through all the vowel sounds on one controlled out-breath.

8.   Choose a note that everyone can reach, and pass it round the circle, increasing in volume as each person picks it up in turn, and then decreasing it. Re-arrange the circle and repeat so that everyone has a go at a different point. (You may need to 'conduct' this.)

9.   Finally, the group walks round the room, independently, each repeating his own name, first softly, then increasing and decreasing at random.

This is a very basic and straightforward exercise routine, designed to make them aware of their voices and how they work, and the breath control which is needed to use them effectively. It is surprising how few people realise that one speaks only on an out-breath, and that speaking or singing are the most efficient use of breath. If you have the vocal skills to lead them (or even better, get one of the group to do so) singing rounds and similar repetitive group songs is valuable and enjoyable. Tongue-twisters encourage vocal dexterity, while rapping and other rhythmic uses of the voice give experience in the making of different vocal patterns. Much depends on the nature of the group and the ages of its members when you are choosing material and techniques to help them flex their vocal muscles.

One exercise which combines rhythm and voice is based on chanting. Divide the group into four, and give each section a line of a chant. These can be made up easily, can be complete nonsense, or tied to a theme. Some examples:-

pineapples and oranges
peaches and pears and gooseberries
melons grapes and tangerines
ripe squashy bananas

rum tum tum tum
ay takki takki ta
oo walla walla woo
eeeeee pop

Each group practises its part of the chant independently, adding clapping and other non-verbal vocal sounds for greater effect. They are then brought back into a circle and the elements are worked into a chanted round, each group repeating its own section as part of the whole.

Whatever methods you employ in vocal work, the aim should be to develop confidence in the use of the voice, and awareness and control of the sounds made when they speak or sing. It is important to avoid anything that smacks of the elocution lesson, however. Local dialect and regional accents should be cherished, and if you can encourage clarity and confidence you will help in maintaining them.

Concentration and observation

The ethos and character of a group, and its ability to progress in its work, can be affected by its ability to concentrate, both singly and collectively, on whatever task is in hand as well as on broader objectives. The ability to observe accurately is closely linked with this. If you can develop these powers within individuals and the group as a whole, you will find that working with them becomes easier and more enjoyable.

As with every workshop exercise and game, it helps the process greatly if you explain why they are asked to engage in a particular activity, its value to them individually and as a group, and its relevance to the work you are doing together. Otherwise, some of these activities can appear to be put into the programme of work simply to fill in time, although realistically this can sometimes happen, without detracting greatly from their intrinsic value!

One of the advantages of playing games which have a purpose in your work is that many of them are familiar, both to you and to the group. They will probably remember playing them when younger, though it does appear nowadays children play far fewer games than they did before the advent of television, and for many they may be new. Either way, it is unlikely that adolescents would play such games unless asked to do so for a particular purpose, but they always seem to do so with enormous enjoyment.

The ones listed here are generally well-known and require little explanation, and you may well know others yourself.

Dragon's Treasure
The players sit in a circle, with one person in the middle,

blindfolded. An object, preferably one that will make a noise such as a bunch of keys, is thrown into the circle. Nominated players in turn attempt to retrieve the treasure, and the 'dragon' has to prevent this by pointing accurately in the direction from which he can hear the sound of movement.

Thief and Guard

A variant on the above. The circle of seated players is broken at one point, which represents the doorway. The blindfolded guard has a 'weapon', such as a rolled newspaper, and his objective is to strike the thief with this before he can recover the treasure and get it back through the door.

You can also play this with the thief blindfolded as well as the guard, and the persons sitting in the circle have the task of gently stopping either thief or guard from colliding with the circle, or breaking through it.

This can be the first stage of a more advanced acting exercise, in which no blindfolds are used, but the players imagine they are in the dark. The group observes the kind of movements which are made both with and without the blindfold, analysing the different ways in which the players move, comparing real blindness to acted blindness.

Big Chief Sitting Bull

The players sit in a circle, all in the same posture. One leaves the room, and another is chosen to lead. The 'on' player comes back and stands in the middle of the circle, with the aim of determining which of the group is leading the series of small movements which all the others follow.

Matthew, Mark, Luke and John

This is a more complex game. The players stand or sit in a circle. They are named as follows: Number One, Matthew, Mark, Luke, John, Two, Three, Four and so on. Together, they clap their hands twice, then click their fingers (or make some other non-vocal noise) twice. This rhythm is sustained throughout the game.

Number One starts, speaking in time to the two claps (e.g.) 'One to Three'. 'Three' answers on the next two claps (e.g.) 'Three to Mark' and so on. The aim is to keep the rhythm steady and for the words to be spoken in time with the two claps, with the only pauses on the second pair of sounds.

If a player named does not reply immediately, keeping the

rhythm, he or she has to move to the last place in the circle on Number One's right, and takes the last number. This changes the numbers of all who were below before, as they now move up a place, and they must be immediately aware of their new numbers.

After each move Number One starts again. Everyone's aim is to get to be Number One. The game has no definite conclusion, and should be played for as long as necessary to establish and maintain the rhythm and concentration.

Salt and Pepper

Players stand in a circle and the leader has two objects. He passes the first to the player on his left, who asks 'What is it?' The reply is 'It's the salt.' This is repeated as the object passes round the circle, and on each move the question is passed back to the leader, and the reply passed back along the line to the questioner. At the same time, the second object is passed similarly to the right... 'It's the pepper.' This appears to be simple until the point at which the objects cross. If the instruction to *always* do the same thing is followed the game can proceed smoothly, and the objects are eventually returned to the leader. Most groups find this virtually impossible the first time they play it, and regard it as a challenge to get it right.

Finally, a quiet activity, useful for bringing down noise and excitement. The group sits or stands in a circle, eyes closed, holding hands. A chosen person gently squeezes the hand of one of those next to him, and this is passed on round the circle. The direction can be changed at will.

The observation activities detailed below can perhaps be better defined as exercises rather than games. The distinction is a somewhat academic one. Both kinds of activities are useful at any stage in the group's work, and in both they can improve performance with practice. The observation exercises are, perhaps, more focused on the acquisition and development of skills, of working in harmony with a partner or a group. Some of these can be developed for specific needs at other stages in your work.

Throwing Mime

Two lines face each other at opposite sides of the room, each person facing a partner. First they mime throwing a tennis ball to each other, then a series of objects of different weight and nature – a shuttlecock, a feather, an egg, a snowball and so on. Establish the need to observe the movements of the partner to determine the response, then ask them to change the 'objects' at random.

Chinese Whispers Mime
The group stands in a circle. Two people face each other, the others have their backs turned. One performs a simple mime to the other, either an abstract set of movements or something definite, such as threading a needle. The second repeats the mime to the third, and so on. The aim should be to achieve an exact reproduction of the first mime round the circle, though this rarely happens.

Walking and copying
The group walks at random around the room. Each person chooses another to observe and attempt to reproduce his movements, balance, bodily stance.

Mirror Work
Pairs face each other. One leads with simple, flowing movements of the hands, arms and body, using different levels and planes. The other copies exactly, as a mirror image. It is useful to use music as a background to this exercise. With practice and experience, the point will come when neither consciously leads, both move in shared harmony. This kind of synchronised movement work can be carried out in larger groups, once the exercise is familiar.

Copy-Cat
Create a simple set. It need be no more than a couple of chairs, perhaps a table or a block. One person goes into the acting area and uses it as he wishes, a second is sent in to join and interact with him. This is non-verbal work. At an appropriate moment, freeze the action. A second pair then tries to reproduce exactly the actions they have observed.

A variation on this exercise is to use a small group, four or five persons, and give them a situation to play in mime, for instance choosing books in a library, trying on clothes in a shop, waiting at a 'bus stop, in a café or a waiting room, candidates in an examination hall. They can also be given a dominant characteristic, such as *anxiety, confidence, depression, cheerfulness*. In the observing group, one person watches one performing person. Again, freeze the action at the right moment, and ask the observers to try to reproduce exactly what they saw.

In both cases, talk over the exercise with the group, helping them to analyse how they carried it out.

Ensemble Work

It is useful at an early stage to practise some simple activities which aim to establish a group awareness, and through which the members can begin to create a group identity through ensemble work. This does not diminish individual creativity and choice, rather it enhances it by directing independent effort towards a specific kind of activity in which the whole can be greater than the sum of its parts.

The exercises given here are fairly simple, but can be adapted to make more complex demands on an established group.

Lines (All these exercises are to be carried out without speaking)

(a) The group forms a line in height order.

(b) A similar line, this time with the smallest in the middle, graduating out to the two tallest at each end.

(c) With 1 January and 31 December at opposite ends of the room, they place themselves in a line according to birth date. No consultation, but check the accuracy when they have finished. This can be surprisingly exact.

There is a multitude of variations which can be devised for the line exercise. The common factor is that they must be done without any consultation.

Shapes, Words and Numbers (Silent again)

(a) Choose a series of different shapes, such as an equal sided square, a rectangle, a right-angled triangle, for the group to create as a whole. This could also be done in pairs or small groups.

(b) According to the size of the group, pick a word and tell them to form it with their bodies.

(c) Give them a series of numbers to create with their bodies.

There may be a tendency for one person to 'direct' these activities. They should be encouraged not to take this easy option.

Tableaux
Give a subject for a tableau. One person takes the initial stance, the others join him to create a physical picture.

Big Machine
One person goes to the middle of the room and repeats a single, mechanical noise and movement. The others join in one by one with their own noises and movements until all are involved.

Many variations are possible. Everyone can start at the same time in different parts of the room, gradually moving together. Sound and movement can be speeded up and slowed down, people can move away and return, the sounds and movements can be changed, or a gradual fusion can take place until everyone is moving in the same way and making the same sound.

Finding Focus
Using a ball or a bean-bag, initiate a game of running catch, in which the thrower calls the name of the catcher. Each time the ball is caught, the whole group freezes and focuses on the catcher for a count of three, in silence, then continues.

Group Movement
The group stands in one corner of the room, in physical contact with each other. On the instruction, they run together around the room as a group, everyone responding to the general direction which is being taken.

Keep this moving fairly fast. Vary it by telling them that they are either running away from, or towards, something or someone. Observe and discuss the different impressions which are given.

Flying Shuttles
Everyone stands at random around the sides of the room, and pairs make eye contact with each other. When the contact is made, they run as fast as possible to change places, avoiding bumping into anyone who is moving across their path.

Energy releasing games

Many of the activities described here are inherently energy releasing, but it is useful to keep in reserve some vigorous, non-demanding games to use in different circumstances. As with all other activities, they should be used for a purpose, not as a stopgap.

In a school situation, a group coming from classroom lessons can be physically sluggish, and a short burst of activity at the beginning of a session can make them more alert and responsive before you go on to more concentrated work. Likewise, a long session in which a lot of concentration has been necessary needs a respite and changed activity at the end, or even halfway through. The placing of such games in a session does need to be carefully judged, because at the wrong time and with the wrong people they can be disruptive. Like so much of this work, it is largely a matter of instinctive response to the group and the situation. And within the vigorous activity, the physical well-being of every member of the group must be respected, as it is in all other work.

Groups tend to develop favourite games, which they will play over and over again, and taking part in these and learning how they are played is a useful initiation for new members of the group.

These are a few suggestions. You will probably know many more of the same and different kinds, and the group can be asked for its ideas – they will probably be offered anyway.

Tag Games

● *Stick in the Mud.* When tagged, stand with feet apart until someone crawls between your legs to release you.

● *Cat and Mouse.* Players form a grid, holding hands in lines. One player is chased by another along the lines. On a signal, the alignment is changed by holding hands in the other direction.

● *Circle Tag.* Players stand in a circle in pairs, one behind another. One player is chased by another, and can escape by standing in front of a pair, releasing the one at the back to be chased.

● *Touch Back Tag.* In facing pairs, each attempts to touch the small of the back of his partner, while protecting his own by fast footwork and bodily evasion. A variation is to have a scarf or handkerchief tucked into the waist at the back which has to be captured.

The Chair Game

Chairs are placed in a circle, one fewer than the number of players. The player 'on' is in the middle. Players agree to swap places by eye

contact. Once it has been made they are committed to change. The
'on' player has to get to a vacant chair. This can be varied by using
slow motion, hopping, crawling, walking backwards, and so on.

Rabid Bunnies
Everyone squats down and hops around the room like a rabbit.
Everyone's aim is to floor another player, by catching him or her
with a foot at the back of the knee. When floored, the player has to
lie on his back on the floor, wave his arms and legs around, scream
a bit, and can then continue. A very silly game, but these are
sometimes the best!

   Many of these games can serve a further purpose. When in the
process of rehearsals, or engaged in character work, such games
can be played in character. They can also be played while running
through a section of script, or using a variety of different emotions,
relationships and motivations, thus extending the whole concept of
'play'.
   Within the limitations of one section of one book, only a small
selection of games, exercises and strategies which can be used as
preliminary work can be described. There are many possibilities for
development and adaptation of those given here, and some are
more appropriate for some groups and circumstances than others.
   It is important not to abandon what may seem to be basic work
as the group develops. Much of it is made more valuable by
repetition at different stages and times, and the charm of the
familiar should not be forgotten. There are also recognisable links
and lines of development between this work and what will be dealt
with later in this book, and when constructing a single workshop
session, a short course, or planning a more extended work, choice
and selections can be made to fit into an overall plan.

Chapter 2
Improvisation

Man is a games-playing animal. All young animals play games: it is an essential part of the growing process, through which they learn to understand the world in which they live and their places in it. Games which develop physical strength and abilities, and games which establish status, are common to all young animals when they come together in groups. In the case of man, who has a more complex society to deal with, and who has the power of speech, these games are more varied and elaborate, and when young children play together their games are often based on mimesis. 'Let's pretend – we're doctors and nurses – cops and robbers – spacemen – teachers and pupils – mothers and fathers.'

In the theatre, the game of 'Let's pretend' is elevated into a complex art form. 'Let's pretend – we're Hamlet and Ophelia – Faust and Mephistopheles – Antigone and Creon – Vladimir and Estragon.'

In the controlled situation of a drama class or a youth theatre group, the adoption of roles and the exploration of situations is at a remove from the spontaneous play of young children. Most adolescents have developed a self-consciousness which precludes an uninhibited approach to the game of 'Let's pretend'. But the more mature attributes of informed choice and analysis which they have acquired at this stage in their lives are ones which can be used to advantage in developing the skills of improvisation.

Improvisation has a central place in most drama work in schools, and is the basis of most youth theatre work. It has equal importance in open workshop sessions and in approaches to scripted work. It frees the imagination, and at the same time directs it towards the achievement of a desired effect. It is the central point in the continuum between 'let's play mothers and fathers' and 'let's play Hamlet and Ophelia', and it faces in both directions, towards the spontaneity of childhood play and the discipline of performance. It builds confidence in individuals, and in the group, giving everyone an awareness of the importance of the part he plays in the shared activity, and a sensitivity and control in his reactions to what is going

on. Thus each member of the group will begin to feel able to depend
on every other person he is working with.

The ability to improvise may be innate, but the skills involved in
successful work of this kind need to be taught, and learned. There
is a validity and freshness in the immediate response, but when a
group is working together the creativity and self-expression of each
person must be controlled and developed to achieve the greater
effect. Therefore the group leader has two tasks of equal
importance. The first is to help the individual to overcome any
inhibitions in self-expression and response to the given situation so
that the imagination may be released. The second is to encourage
an awareness of group cooperation in order to bring about the
desired aim, which is to sustain an idea, develop it, and bring it to a
satisfying conclusion.

There are two distinct stages in improvisation work. The first is
purely process, the second moves towards product. The first
demands an immediate response to a given situation or stimulus,
and although in some cases the work can be developed into
something which can be watched (and at times it is useful to
incorporate this as part of the learning process) its main function is
to enable the acquisition and practice of a variety of skills. The
second builds on the first, and usually involves a pair or group
working together to explore a theme and dramatise it, eventually
showing the results to the rest of the group.

Both kinds of activities have their place in each stage of the group's
work. It can be tempting to abandon the first stage after a few sessions
on the basis of 'they've done that – they know it – they'll be bored
doing it again'. But the earlier exercises, chosen with relevance to the
major work you want to do in a session are, like the warm-up
exercises, of continuing value in developing the skills and confidence
of the group, and also help the integration of any new members. They
gain pleasure from repeating the familiar, and finding that they can
perform certain exercises with greater ease, extending their inherent
possibilities. And they will approach the demands of more developed
and finished work with greater confidence.

The second stage, while drawing on the skills learned in the first,
gives them the opportunity to try out approaches to the
dramatisation of themes and situations. Whereas in the first stage
any theme or topic chosen is best to be simple and mundane, the
second stage can make greater demands on their imaginations and
performing abilities, moving perhaps into the abstract. But here too
there are different strategies available for choosing material, and for

approaches to the given task, which will be discussed later.

For the first stage, some of the exercises are purely physical, while others involve speech. It is best to begin simply and gradually introduce more complex and demanding work. The larger the group working as a unit on an improvisation the more difficult it is for them to work effectively, so the unit size should be built up over time, although in the early stages it is possible to use the group as a whole for certain exercises.

The basic skills of improvisation

Action/reaction (pair work)
Player A takes up a bodily position and holds it. B reacts to the position with an appropriate action and holds the final position. A says 'thank you' and reacts in turn to B's position, who says 'thank you' and so on. With practice, a flow of movement can develop between the partners.

This may be a little difficult to envisage, so the following example might help. Player A may bend down as if lifting a heavy box. B helps lift it onto an imaginary surface, holding a final position upright with hands apart – he or she could be holding a tray with crockery on it. A takes plates from the tray and stacks them on a shelf. B takes the plate being held by A and changes it into a book, opens it and so on.

They should be encouraged not to worry about what specifically is being done in each action, but simply to perform a movement which responds to what is suggested by the partner's bodily position. Saying 'thank you' acknowledges that the physical offer has been accepted, and this underlines the fundamental rule for successful improvisation – always accept the offer.

Moulding a statue (pair work)
Player A is the artist, B is a piece of clay. A moulds B gently into the shape desired, concentrating on every aspect of the body, such as position of feet, hands and fingers, expression, angle of head, body shape. They should be encouraged not to try to put their partners into positions which are uncomfortable. As with the previous exercise, with practice a flow of movement and interaction between the two bodies (in this case one active and one passive) can be achieved. Background music can be used to accompany this exercise.

Meeting/Greeting/Parting (pair work)

The instruction is to devise a limited set of movements through which two people meet, greet each other, and part. Ten or twelve movements should be sufficient.

This basic exercise can be used with a number of variations. It can be played using different speeds, run backwards and forwards (like a film), or a limited script can be introduced. One variation is that one of the pair thinks he recognises the other, only to find that he is greeting a stranger, and retreats in embarrassment.

Using bench or screen (pairs or threes)

This is a rather more advanced exercise. Using a simple focal point, such as a bench or a screen, the aim is to introduce a quality of surprise into the actions. To work well this does need an ad hoc audience to respond.

The instruction is simply to use the object and a limited space around it in unexpected ways. Played seriously, whole scenarios can develop, and when they have had a little time to experiment with the idea, spontaneous work should be presented to the audience.

Photographic assignment (pairs and larger groups)

This exercise enables you to move from pair work to the involvement of a much larger group. The starting point is similar to *moulding a statue* but in this instance one person is a photographer, the other a model. The photographer places a model in a series of poses and chooses the best angle to photograph from. Steer them away from the idea of fashion or pin-up photography. A theme can be given, to encourage a coherent set of poses.

Then move on to whole-group activity. Split them into groups of three or four, each of which is to act as a team of photographers with an assignment to make a series of photographs of a particular event, or on a theme. Each team of photographers has the whole of the rest of the group as available material. They must plan the pictures they want to take, and how they will position the rest of the group. You may need pens and paper for the planning stage.

Each group in turn then arranges its series of pictures. Once they have positioned everyone to their satisfaction, they can look at the scene from a variety of angles, noting how the relationships between the bodies alter according to where they are viewed from.

If you happen to have a polaroid camera available for them to use it provides an extra dimension to this exercise.

This is a valuable exercise at quite an early stage in improvisation work. It encourages cooperation, thinking about what they wish to achieve, the skills of telling a story in pictures. You may wish to suggest themes to them, but it is often best to leave it to them to choose. They can create powerful and serious images, and as no speech is required except in the planning stage the work enables everyone to participate without the more extrovert dominating the process.

Taking an emotion into a space (individual and group)

This again is a non-verbal activity, involving the whole group, in this case with a few working at one time, while the others observe.

Create an acting area and a minimal set of two or three chairs or blocks. Each person in turn is given an emotion to take into the space, and the instructions are to use the set, the space, and to interact with anyone else who comes into it. You can use emotions such as *fear, happiness, anger, uncertainty, pleasure,* and so on. Send one person in, then add one or two more at intervals, each with his or her own emotion. As the work is non-verbal, they must demonstrate physically the given emotion. When they reach what seems the appropriate point in their interaction, freeze the action, or ask them to find a final position and hold it. Discuss with the rest of the group what they saw taking place.

This exercise helps them to be aware of the space they are using, of expressing feelings and interacting with others without using words. Surprisingly extended and satisfying scenarios can develop without any pre-planning. This is improvisation stripped down to the basic situation of a number of persons working together within a given space. Because there is no dialogue, the process is less stressful to the more inhibited, while the extroverts can express themselves fully but within a restricted compass. From your knowledge of the group, you should be able to choose the right emotion for the right person, and this can sometimes be the one which is directly opposite to his or her own dominant characteristic.

You will want to bring in verbal exercises at quite an early stage, probably using them alongside the non-verbal activities. Here again, cooperation between small and larger groups is the foundation on which you can build more demanding work.

Successful and satisfying spontaneous improvisation can only be achieved if people have assimilated (albeit unconsciously in some cases) the groundrules that apply to this work. Once they have done so their ability to create, sustain and develop an improvised situation can be limitless. I have known groups of young people run twelve-hour non-stop improvisation sessions with confidence, energy (though there is usually a lull around hours six and seven) and what seems an unlimited supply of ideas.

There are two major problems which occur when you begin to use speech in improvisation. These are drying up, and blocking. Blocking means that the improvisation cannot move forward or develop in any interesting way because one, or more, of the people working do not accept the verbal offers which are made, answering monosyllabically, or failing to develop possible lines of dialogue and situation. The following exercises are designed to help overcome these problems. The aim is to achieve successful cooperation and interaction between pairs, and within larger groups.

Open the box (pairs)

This exercise should create non-stop speech from one of the pair, with encouragement from the other. Each pair sits facing one another, with an imaginary box between them. Player A takes things from the box, one after another as quickly as possible, saying what each one is – the first thing that comes to mind. 'It's a whale–a pair of spectacles – an orange – a hat – a rainforest – a bunch of flowers.' Player B encourages enthusiastically, but without prompting or suggesting the name of the object. This should run for about two or three minutes before they change over.

Giving presents (pairs)

Player A gives B a present in a box. The only indication of what it is, is the size and weight of the imaginary box, and A should not plan what it is. B opens the box, takes out the gift, says what it is and uses it (puts on the necklace, rides the bicycle). Player B tells A how much he or she likes the present, and in turn gives A a present and so on.

Showing round the room (pairs)

Player A takes B for a guided tour round a room in his or her house, talking about the things which are there, giving a verbal picture of the room and its contents. The room should be either his space, or one which he feels most at home in. Then B does the same for A.

A development of this exercise is for each person to choose an object which he found particularly interesting from the other's room, and each pair then devises a short improvisation involving both objects.

As in each of these exercises the pairs are working independently and simultaneously, you may wish to pause from time to time to let them share their experiences with the whole group, asking them to talk about the most unusual object taken from the box, the best present received, the most interesting things in the room.

Just a minute (solo)
This encourages a flow of speech and ideas. A number of topics are decided on, and each person in turn has to speak for one minute on a given topic. Instead of penalising hesitation or repetition, encouragement is given by one member of the group (or the group as a whole). The instructions 'expand', 'contract' or 'go on' are used, to stimulate speech and influence the way the topic is presented. Play this using the whole group as the audience.

Commentary (pairs or threes)
A simple situation is given which involves a task, such as washing the dog, painting a door, putting up a tent. In each group, one person provides a commentary as the task is performed. Like *Just a minute*, a flow of speech is the aim, in a more organised fashion than in the earlier exercises, as the commentators have to define, describe, and communicate with an audience.

The preceding exercises stimulate a flow of ideas which are put into speech, and also to a certain extent verbal interaction. The following suggestions are for exercises which are designed to help overcome problems of blocking, and encourage awareness of the need to allow each person involved in an improvisation to speak without being interrupted.

One to fifty (pairs)
Give a simple scenario, such as a parent confronting a child returning home late, boy chatting up girl (or vice versa). The instruction is to play the scene using numbers, counting from one to fifty, each person taking up the next number consecutively, and

using as many or as few numbers as necessary. As they do not have to think of the words, they can play the scene concentrating on the situation and the motivations of the characters, and there is a built-in termination point which helps to shape the development.

You can, alternatively, use the alphabet or nonsense language, but the pre-determined termination is always useful to enable them to control what they are doing.

Having established relationship and mood in this way, the scene can be replayed using words. As the group becomes more experienced, you can increase the number of people involved in this exercise, but it is seldom successful played with more than four.

Two as one (pairs and whole group)

Begin with pairs. They should construct a monologue, building it up by using one word each, using only the pronoun 'I' – never 'we'. A topic can be suggested to get them going. Once this has been established and a flow of speech achieved, the pair links arms, joins another pair, and conducts a conversation with them, each pair speaking as if it is one person. The exercise can be developed by giving the whole group a situation, such as a party, an airport lounge or similar location, and allowing them to interact freely.

This is not an easy exercise, but it is worth persevering with, as it encourages sensitivity and awareness of the need to cooperate.

Chain Reaction (group)

This is an exercise which can be introduced at a fairly early stage, but which is also useful as a warm-up with an established group, as it improves greatly with experience.

The group sits in a circle, leaving a large acting space in the middle. One person comes into the centre and takes a pose. A second joins him, reacts physically and verbally to the pose, and they improvise freely from that point. Let the action run until you see the right point to freeze it. On the command the action is held, and the first player leaves. Another comes in and reacts to the position of the remaining player, producing a new improvisation.

You need to run this quite fast. Don't let a flagging improvisation run into the ground, nor be tempted to let a fluent pair run on too long. Aim to involve everyone in the group in turn.

There are a number of variations on this exercise, which can be introduced as the group becomes more experienced. One is to put together a list of possibilities under the headings of character, location and situation. Playing with the above format, the first pair is told who they are, where they are, and the situation they have to play. For example, a policeman and a tramp, at a railway station, during the rush hour. When the action is frozen, extra characters can be introduced and others removed, and the other elements changed when appropriate.

When using this variation, it is likely that each action will run for longer than in the simpler version, but, again, the aim is to keep it moving quickly and freezing it at any sign of flagging to bring about a change of direction from a new stimulus.

Styles of playing can be added as an extra element for the more experienced, such as silent movie, melodrama, soap opera, Shakespearian tragedy.

Strategies for extended improvisation

All the exercises described previously encourage and depend on spontaneity. They build physical and verbal confidence, and establish working methods and cooperation within a group. The nature of the material which is used to trigger responses should be simple, but it need not be banal.

A common initial reaction from young people when faced with the task of improvising is to go for comedy. This can be a defence mechanism, and it is a very understandable one. Everyone is sensitive to laughter, and its ability to damage. If a young person is laughed at when he is attempting to do something serious, he will be disheartened, embarrassed, and reluctant to try again. Conversely, laughter can indicate admiration and acceptance when it is deliberately sought. This is the easier option, and the one which many people choose.

Comedy has its place and should not be discouraged, especially in the early stages, but an individual or a group which aims for nothing more than a cheap laugh is going for an easy and extremely limiting option. You can end up with a group which has a kind of comedy hierarchy. Some people have a natural gift for producing a comic effect, and are genuinely funny. They tend to be admired by others, who try to emulate them, with varying success. In such an environment, a number of blocks occur which create a major barrier to development. The most confident are rewarded for what they do most easily, the less so strive for similar rewards. In both cases limitations are being reinforced which prejudice the achievement of demanding and satisfying work. Comedy should be valued where it is appropriate, but not the extent that it becomes the dominant, or in the worst cases, the only genre.

How to overcome this probem? A lot depends on the nature of the group, your relationship with it, and the leading personalities within it. It is no use demanding a non-comic approach from a group in which this kind of playing has become established as the norm. It is easier with a new group, to which you can make clear that to play a situation and bring out its serious aspects is difficult, but very worthwhile. Such attempts should always be praised, even when they do not fully achieve what they set out to do. At the same time the group should be encouraged always to accept generously what any of its members offer, whether suggestions, ways of working or finished product. If you give the lead in this, you will help establish an atmosphere of mutual support and interest in the whole range of possible approaches to improvisation. And if you can get the more dominant people in the group interested in extending their personal range you will have gone a long way towards overcoming the problem.

One way to tackle it is to meet the challenge head-on. You will be introducing more developed improvisation exercises at quite an early stage, to allow them to practise their skills and express their own ideas. When doing so, you can give them a theme around which to create a developed improvisation, to show to the rest of the group, with the instruction to take two completely contrasting approaches, one comic and one serious. When both have been shown, discuss them and help the group to analyse the relative merits and successes, or failures, of both. The opportunity to analyse finished work, or work in progress, helps them to make judgements about what they are doing, and, over time, this feeds back into their own working processes.

As the group develops and consolidates its skills in improvisation, you can introduce more varied and demanding tasks. The two types of work should continue to be used, that is pure process, and process leading to product. Vary the work by using different combinations, from individual work, to pairs and larger groups. They should now be used to working before an 'audience' and watching others work, so that it becomes possible to use some exercises as demonstrations without losing their interest.

A useful demonstration exercise is one in which a short script is given to a pair to begin an improvisation. They should use this to establish the beginning of the action, then develop it and bring it to a natural conclusion. The short script can be completely neutral in tone and content, so that the following action is left completely open. Or it can present a situation, a relationship, or a focus. The following are examples of each of these.

neutral
Hello.
Hello.
Do you know what time it is?
Yes, it's half past six.

situation
Excuse me, is this the waiting room?
Yes.
Do you mind if I sit down?
No, there's plenty of room.

relationship
I'm, just going out for a bit.
Oh, no.
What's the matter?
Do you have to?

focus
Hey, look over there!
Where?
Over there, to the right.
What is it?

Each of these openings gives rise to a great number of possibilities, some fairly mundane, but as members of the group become confident in self-expression, and know that they can depend on others to accept the offers they make in improvisation, their development of these simple openings can move in any direction. Thus improvisation can become surreal, fantastic: the players can establish recognisable relationships between the characters they assume, and explore these relationships. Discourage any pre-planning, this is pure improvisation. Encourage them to accept and build on the ideas their partners are offering in the course of playing. Be ready to cut any work that flags or goes on for too long, or is becoming self-indulgent, and discuss any difficulties which occurred, as well as what made a particular improvisation successful.

If you want to give a fictional location for this kind of exercise it is, again, preferable to go for the ordinary. The more complex or restrictive the location is the more built-in limitations present themselves. Use places such as 'bus queues, a park bench, library, café, pub, railway station. Alternatively, an event can be chosen, such as a party, school reunion, job interview, formal meeting. In these cases you can introduce more players, but the more that are introduced the more difficult it becomes to sustain an instant improvisation unless they are quite experienced.

Instant improvisations using the whole group can be great fun. You do need some planning and structuring to prevent them becoming chaotic. The group should be reminded of your control mechanism (the command 'freeze') before they start. Unlike the short script exercises, the given situation does need built-in limitations, so that ideas can be developed within the defined parameters.

A simple situation, which provides many possibilities, is the marketplace. About a third of the group are stall-holders, the rest are the general public. Give them time to set up and establish the action, and then you can develop it along a variety of lines by feeding in different stimuli.

You can alter the course of the action by giving confidential instructions to individuals or a group of players, either before or during the run of the action. Here are some suggestions:

● one player is a trading standards officer;
● one is a pick-pocket;
● one is a plain-clothes policeman;
● one faints;
● several are foreigners who cannot speak English;
● the marketplace is in a foreign country and the shoppers are tourists;
● one trader is a newcomer who takes over the pitch of an established trader who arrives late;
● some are buskers, beggars, and so on.

They should all be instructed to be aware of and respond to what is going on around them and, as when working in smaller groups, to accept the ideas offered and help them develop.

Depending on how well it is running, you can give this exercise a good length of time to develop. You may also wish to build in other strategies which will help them to be aware of what is going on, such as freezing the action at certain stages, allowing one group to continue and develop what they are doing while the others observe, and then re-starting the general action from the point at which the isolated action ended.

Other locations which can be used in this way are a large railway station, an airport lounge, a hotel reception area. They need to be chosen to give scope for bringing together a wide variety of people: the disco, school playground or classroom are really too restricting.

Another strategy for whole-group work is to create a community, such as a street, block of flats, village, small town, and allow them to choose their own roles and relationships as inhabitants. Then provide a reason for bringing the whole community together, such as a public meeting or a celebration of some kind. This can then be run in much the same way as the marketplace exercise, providing additional stimuli as the action develops.

A different kind of whole-group exercise is one of the many variations on *Master and Servant*. One player is the master (it is best to choose neither the over-confident nor the too retiring for this role). The rest of the group sit in a circle or at one end of the room facing the master. The master can pick any person to perform a real or imaginary task, such as telling jokes, scratching the master's back, sweeping the floor, preparing a meal. As the action develops, more servants are called in. The basic rule is that the servants must obey the master without question. If any servant displeases in any way he or she is instantly 'dead'. Servants may take the risk of making fun of the master, but if this is seen they are liable to be 'killed' or have to pay a forfeit. This open-ended exercise can become chaotic, and you need to ensure that unreasonable or dangerous tasks are not attempted. It seldom has a natural conclusion, though it has been known to result in a palace revolution in which the master is deposed.

All these exercises concentrate on process. When you wish to move on to prepared work, the most satisfying experiences and the best results are often based on ideas which come from the group itself, and it is possible to discover themes and ideas which arise from the group working together on creating material.

One strategy is to invent a character, and take it through a number of situations. The group sits in a circle and one person is nominated to start, with a definition of the gender of the person. 'There was once a girl.' The next person gives her name, the next begins to describe her, and each person in turn gives other facts about her, her age, where she lives, what she does. Move on to events in her life, relationships, ambitions, and how she faces up to challenges. You will probably have to intervene with some questions from time to time to push the story forward. A conclusion may be reached, or the story can be open-ended.

The group is then split into smaller groups to dramatise the material they have jointly produced. If it was inconclusive, one group can be given the task of producing a final episode. The prepared improvisations are then run in sequence, with a different person from each group taking on the role of the main character in each section.

A similar strategy for finding material is *one-word-at-a-time*. It can be useful to run this once with the whole group as a demonstration, and then split into smaller groups to collect the material for improvisation. Going round the circle, each person in turn supplies a consecutive word in a narrative. The only proviso is that it would make some grammatical sense, but they should be encouraged to say the first word that comes to mind. The story should not go on too long, and one member of each group should write it down as it develops. The resulting narrative is used as the basis for improvisation. The whole of the text does not have to be used, but the key elements identified and dramatised. This can result in some marvellously surreal work, and helps to overcome any self-limitation to the literal and naturalistic.

Another exercise which can encourage a non-naturalistic (and therefore more dramatically exciting) approach is the limited script. Split the group into smaller sections, provide them with pencils and paper, and ask them to find ten words to be used by another group as a script. The words can be as disparate as they like, but should be mainly nouns, verbs, adjectives and adverbs. Each group then prepares an improvisation on the script given to them by another group, using only those words as dialogue, in any order, and repeated as often as necessary.

Ideas for improvisation can also come from discussion. With the group sitting in a circle, introduce a strong, possibly emotive word, such as *fear, success, authority, equality*. Everyone has the opportunity to say what the words mean to him. These reactions are discussed and then in smaller groups they produce improvisations which incorporate some of the ideas they have shared.

Two words which produce some interesting reactions are *heaven* and *hell*. You need to ask them what the words mean to them in a metaphorical sense. When moving on to work on this material, you can ask groups to prepare two improvisations, one in which they use their word in its literal sense, and one in which it is used metaphorically.

A light-hearted improvisation session can be based on traditional material, stories such as *Cinderella, Jack and the Beanstalk,* and so on. Ask for a dramatisation of the story in a particular style. The styles you suggest will depend on the nature and the experience of the group, but there is a wide possible range – non-verbal, as a Western, a silent movie, a soap opera, a Shakespearean tragedy, a television documentary, a pop video. Make sure they do know the stories (ask them to suggest titles) and do not choose those with an overcomplex story line.

Though the material in such work is not particularly serious or thought-provoking, this does enable them to concentrate on selection, presentation, and style. As in many of the exercises, you should encourage them to identify the key episodes in a story, and concentrate on these, while not ignoring the fundamental requirement, which is to put the story across to the audience.

A rich source of material is the immediate experience of the members of the group, especially of their own families. This should not be used in an obvious way, simply providing subjects for role-play, because this can often yield little more than two-dimensional, stereotyped playing. As preparation, ask the group to observe their parents, their siblings, their grandparents and other members of the older generation, and to identify a typical gesture or remark. These can be used in free-flowing, abstract improvisations, with the gestures repeated and exaggerated, performed at different speeds, broken down into their components. The words and phrases can be similarly used. Patterns of movement and sound will emerge, from which small groups can construct their own improvisations.

This purely abstract expression can be incorporated into more realistic work. Reminiscences can be collected from members of different generations, perhaps of one event from different individual perspectives. Personal, local and national histories and events can be explored in this way, with the current generation playing themselves in the context of the experience and history of their families, possibly looking forward to the next generation, in an invented future.

It is impossible to attempt to include here all the possible material which can be used as stimulus for prepared improvisations, and I have concentrated more on approaches to gathering material. Almost anything can be used as stimulus: newspaper articles and headlines, local and current events, social issues, poetry, or extracts from novels or plays, a single object, or a number of seemingly unrelated objects. Imaginary situations, with some event or individual acting as a catalyst, can produce exciting work, such as a group stranded in a mountain hut in a snowstorm, a revolutionary group in hiding from authority, prisoners in a cell awaiting interrogation.

What is essential, however, is that in the first places time and space are allowed for discussion and the sharing of ideas, and then, once the ideas have been explored verbally, they begin almost immediately to try out their ideas dramatically. Do it, don't talk about it. Give time limits for preparation, and indicate a realistic length for the finished product, otherwise you can get (at one end of the spectrum) a thirty-second last-minute offering from a group which has spent too much time talking about what they might do rather than trying out their ideas, at the other a self-indulgent, rambling and formless piece which lasts for far too long.

If you establish at an early stage a discipline for working on prepared improvisations, you, and they, will find that the quality of both the process and the product is increasingly satisfactory. Of course there will be failures, overambitious ideas which are unsustainable, groups which hit a block, but these can be put to good use in any discussion of why some things did not work.

Story-telling

Some of the exercises already detailed touch on the skills of story-telling, but it is something which stands in its own right, and you may wish to spend some time concentrating on its techniques, and exploring its possibilities for performance. Story-telling has the advantage that, in its simplest forms, it can be presented as performance with a minimum of technical back-up. It is one of the earliest forms of dramatic expression, and basically it requires no more than the teller and the audience. It is found in every culture, and though in the more sophisticated societies it suffered a decline, there are signs that it is making a comeback.

Story-telling is central to any dramatic performance, from the simplest level to the most complex. Perhaps the most useful instruction to be given to any group of actors preparing a play is that they must tell the story. However interesting and entertaining the style and techniques of a performance, what the audience wants to know is what happens next and how it will be resolved. If the story is a familiar one, the audience will still be gripped by the detail of its telling. Traditional material, and recognised conventions of story-telling, still have the power to entertain. Mastery of this art can give young people confidence in their powers of expression, which will benefit them in many aspects of their lives, apart from the use they can make of this skill in the more specialised area of drama work.

The following exercises offer a variety of approaches to developing story-telling techniques, and some suggestions for the use of these in performance. For some of these exercises, you may find it an advantage to give them notice of the material you will be working on in the next session, so that they have the opportunity to think about it beforehand. If you have a culturally mixed group, there will be many opportunities to share material which may be unfamiliar to some people. In all these exercises, the listening is as active as the telling.

Personal stories (pairs and group)

Prepare them in advance by asking them to think about something that happened to them when they were small children.

In pairs, each tells the other his personal story. As far as possible, this should be done without interruption, though they can be instructed to ask questions if anything is unclear, or if the account flags. The stories should be limited to a telling-time of three to four minutes.

When the stories have been exchanged, each pair swaps partners with another pair, and each again tells a story, but this time it is the one he has been told, not his own, and it should be told as if it happened to him.

By now, everyone in the group will have three stories, his own, and those of two other people. Bring them back into one large group, sitting in a circle, and ask for a selection of stories to be told, which can either be the tellers' personal stories, or ones they have heard. Again, they should all be told in the first person.

When you are story-telling with the whole group, it is useful to set up some formal convention to assist a smooth operation. The simplest is to have an object, a 'story-telling stone', which is passed to the person chosen to speak, and while he holds it he has the floor. It can be passed from hand to hand around the circle, or

given at random to another person, or it can be requested by
anyone who wishes to speak giving an agreed signal.

Interview (pairs)

This can be prepared to show to others, or can be carried out
spontaneously. It works most successfully when done by one pair
with the rest of the group acting as an audience.

One person is the interviewer, the other someone who has
carried out an imaginary exploit, which can be as dramatic or as
ridiculous as you choose. Possibilities are:-

- climbing solo the north face of the Post Office Tower (or
  anything else);
- conducting a survey on the culinary preferences of orang-
  utans;
- swimming the Channel underwater backwards;
- researching the possible uses of wildebeest in the Japanese
  motorcycle industry.

However ridiculous or comic the material used, the interview
must be carried out with total seriousness. The audience should not
interrupt the course of questioning, but may be invited to ask
questions and offer comments at the end of the interview. Material
for this exercise should always be chosen with its narrative
possibilities in mind.

Stories in a circle (whole group)

Brief one member of the group to begin the telling of a traditional
story. As first speaker, he holds the story-telling stone, opens the
proceedings by starting the story, breaking off at an appropriate
moment, and passing the stone to the person on his left, who
continues and passes the stone on in his turn. Nobody should
speak for more than about a minute, and if anyone does not know
how to continue the stone should be passed on immediately.

This is one of the contexts in which traditional material from
different cultures can be shared, and if you know that this
possibility exists, you can facilitate it by suggesting in advance
that people can bring stories which they share with some of the
group, but which are unfamiliar to others. Passing the stone from
hand to hand allows the stories to flow easily, even when it has to
be handed on by those who do not know the story being told.

You could thus experience a story-telling session in which

everyone heard (for example) some of the Anansi stories, something from the Ramayana, and some traditional Western folk tales from Celtic, Norse, Germanic or Romance backgrounds. Though the latter may be re-told in the sanitised versions by which children now receive them from cartoon films or Ladybird books, they are still part of a living tradition, and retain some of their original power in the strength of their narratives.

If you want to extend this exercise, you can move on to original stories. By re-telling known stories, the group will have assimilated some of the forms and conventions which make for interesting oral presentation, and these should work their way into any original material which they create. This gives the opportunity for the group to create new stories, based on contemporary culture, with structures drawn from traditional sources.

When asking them to create original stories, you are likely to have to play a more active part. You may need to begin the story yourself, using a conventional opening, and establishing some characters, location, and circumstances. At a crucial moment, hand the stone to anyone in the circle, to continue the story. He in turn can hand it to anyone else.

You will find that some people can continue confidently, but others may require some prompting by leading questions to carry the narrative forward. Be alert for signs of the story reaching a satisfactory conclusion, and encourage this to happen.

This exercise can be carried out by passing the stone round the circle to each in turn, but the random element is an advantage as it prevents people pre-planning for their expected turn, and thereby encourages more active listening in order to be able to react spontaneously.

Solo stories

Find a source of traditional stories which are not familiar to the group, possibly from a non-represented culture. The stories should be quite short and easily memorable, with strong narrative lines. Print a selection of these.

Each person can choose a story from the selection. It does not matter if the same story is told by more than one person. They are asked to prepare the stories for re-telling to an audience, not learning them word-by-word, but selecting the major features which they may wish to stress or elaborate.

Some time and care should be given to this preparation. They can, if they wish, work in pairs or small groups to help each other with suggestions. If it is appropriate, they can find some prop, or piece of costume, to support their presentation.

The stories are then told individually to the rest of the group. If you have a large group, you may wish to spread this activity over more than one session, interspersed with other activities. It is best, however, for the whole group to be involved, rather than splitting into several small groups for the presentation of the stories.

The following are further suggestions for approaches to story-telling:

(a) one person tells a story, while his other partner acts it in mime, playing all the parts;
(b) use a musical accompaniment, which comments on and reflects the action;
(c) narrative and dialogue are split, with the story-teller narrating, and two or three actors supplying the dialogue and limited action;
(d) a group simultaneously tells a story and acts it.

This work can form the basis of a performance, once the group has become familiar with the techniques of holding an audience's attention while telling a story, such as the use of eye contact, limited gesture, the stresses, pauses and repetitions, which are all part of this art. However, if the work is taken on to performance, be careful not to allow it to become too slick and polished. At its most effective, story-telling is immediate, and gives the impression that the tale is being told for the first time – however familiar it may be.

The use of devised work in performance

It is a truism that some of the best work done by youth groups is never seen by an audience. There are occasional moments of pure magic which can occur at any time, in preliminary work as well as more developed exercises. While the intrinsic value of this work for the personal development of the individual and the group is widely recognised and self-justified in emotional, intellectual and spiritual terms, the aspect of performance cannot be ignored, as it is the arts and discipline of the theatre which are being employed, and it is in performance that young people can use the language of the theatre to explore their own, and others' experiences, and communicate directly on their chosen terms.

Work which is solely production-orientated will usually become sterile and limited. The need to attract an audience can determine the choice and nature of the material. But a working programme which incorporates workshop sessions in their own right alongside productions, either major or smallscale, can offer the group members a balanced and exciting experience. They then have the opportunity to share ideas, develop skills, test themselves individually and as members of a group, and also to present their finished work to the wider community, which can be anything from a small, invited audience, to a large, paying, theatre audience.

Devised work, based on improvisation, can be a good choice as a first production for a new group, though it should not be regarded as limited to these early stages, or purely as apprentice work. Indeed, as the group grows in maturity and experience it can be quite capable of producing a first-rate full-length devised play. Nowadays, many professional theatre companies work for all or part of their time in this way.

A new group can gain great confidence from the process of polishing and perfecting their own work and presenting it to an audience. Confidence in performance will be founded on the use of their own words and material, saying what they want to say in the way in which they want to say it. They will also have the opportunity to incorporate their skills in other disciplines, such as music and dance. They will learn how to select, shape and present their ideas to make a coherent whole, which communicates to an audience.

Throughout the workshop sessions, the group will have been engaging in exploration of topics which are important to them. In the suggestions given for exercises, there has not been a great deal of material which may appear to be of immediate and pressing social relevance, not much that is directly linked with youth culture. However sympathetic we, as adults, are to the adolescents we are working with, and however much we may think we are in touch with their world, the fact is that we are outsiders. However much mutual liking and respect there is between a group and its leader, our experience of life is different from theirs in many ways, and we do not always use the same codes.

Our task as teachers, workshop leaders, youth theatre directors, is to enable them to explore their own concerns using the skills and disciplines of the theatre. Thus it is through their approach to any given topic for improvisation, as well as the suggestions which they make, that they bring their own world into the arena, and allow us to share it. Through their approaches to that material, their choice of key issues, the emphasis which they put on certain aspects, the style in which they present it, they are discovering and re-inventing the language of theatre, making it their own, not the preserve of a trained, adult, élite.

It is at this stage that they deserve – and need – to communicate with an audience. They will probably feel this as strongly as you do. The use of devised work for performance is dealt with fully later in this book. It is sufficient here to introduce the idea that, when a series of workshops which may have been based on related or complementary topics has been particularly successful, and the group shows an interest in taking the work further, it may be the right time to think about using some of that material for performance. At the very least, keep a record of what was done, and the approaches to it, as you may find it valuable at a later time.

Chapter 3

Character work

Even the most basic improvisation exercise takes the 'actor' beyond the confines of his own character and experience as he explores and develops a role within a given situation. Although the situation may be familiar, the act of isolating it and focusing on it dramatically makes it new, and the reactions within it may well differ radically from the behaviour in everyday life. Without any deep analysis or preparatory work, he is taking on a new role, and operating in a new way because of the demands of the task undertaken. Improvisation is the essential first stage for more developed character work.

At the earliest stages of improvisation, the characters created are likely to be two-dimensional, or stereotypes, and exciting work can be achieved on this basis. But the point will come in any group's work when its members are ready to go beyond this stage, and sublimate their own identities in those of other, created, fictional characters. This will extend the range of their work, giving it greater depth and interest. They will be able to move beyond the confines of their own experience, society and physical environment. They can thus achieve a greater understanding of other people, see the world from a different perspective, and incorporate that knowledge into their own lives.

One of the most difficult things for an adolescent to undertake in theatre work is to assume the role and persona of another, possibly older, person. But if careful preparation has been done, such performance can be convincing, both to the actor and the audience. Rather than a superficial imitation, or even caricature, the enactment comes from within. The actor may be playing that fictional person experiencing stress, or grief, or delight, but he will also know how that person gets out of bed in the morning, makes a cup of tea, reads a paper. He will know what made that character behave in a certain way under the given circumstances.

Of course, you will not want to undertake detailed character work before every improvisation exercise. It may be entirely inappropriate to the task in hand. It would certainly be time-consuming and inhibit spontaneity. But when members of the group have done work on the creation of character, that experience will inform the work they do on all levels. If you wish to use improvised work in devising a play, character work assumes an even greater importance. And when scripted work is undertaken, they will need to know how to lift the words from the page and integrate speech and action to create a fully understood and developed character.

Work on creating and building characters, like all other drama activities, needs to be approached in logical and easy stages, and should take place alongside the development of skills in improvisation. The two activities are interdependent and complementary.

Preliminary character work

Preliminary character work can start from where and who they are. The following exercises are designed to allow them to isolate and concentrate on aspects of their own physical behaviour, and to observe and analyse that of others, always aiming for the truth in any action.

1.   In their own characters, ask them to mime the performance of a simple action, or to show their behaviour in an everyday situation. If you give them a short time to think before carrying out the exercise, the results are likely to contain more truth.

     Tasks could be

     ● doing the washing-up;
     ● wiring a plug;
     ● making a bed;
     ● making toast;
     ● putting on make-up;
     ● making and drinking a cup of tea;
     ● reading a book or a paper.

     Situations

     ● waiting for a 'bus;
     ● watching television;
     ● sitting in a doctor's or dentist's waiting room;
     ● waiting for an interview with a teacher or employer.

Some of these tasks can be carried out singly, while for others you may wish to use a small group to allow interaction. Speech can also be used if it is appropriate, but at this stage try to avoid any narrative developing, as that may detract from the concentration on behaviour. Let the rest of the group observe and comment on what they see. Is it a truthful reflection of what they know of the people they are watching?

At first, you may well find that there is a tendency to overact, and for an element of self-caricature to creep in. When this happens, stop the exercise and discuss what is happening.

This work can be developed by putting in an additional factor:

● Ask them to repeat it as if they are depressed, happy, in a hurry, on their birthday. Note the differences made to their physical behaviour.

● Ask them to carry out the tasks as if they were another member of the group. Again, help them to avoid caricature, and discuss the results.

● Put the whole group in a situation, such as an examination hall, at a party, on a beach, at a railway station. Then, re-play it, swapping characters.

● Sit one person on a 'park bench' in his own character. Send in another to join him in an assumed character, such as a policeman, tramp, mother, priest. Give them an opening line of dialogue, such as 'What are you doing here?' which either can use, and allow a short development of the situation. Observe the contrast and detail of one person playing himself, another an assumed role.

2. The next stage is to isolate still further aspects of physical behaviour.

(a) Place a chair in the middle of the room and ask one person to sit on it, and to freeze the position when ready. Allow the group a moment to observe the pose, and then discuss what they see. Is the body stiff, or relaxed? Where is he or she looking? Note the position of legs and feet. Are they relaxed, or in a position that indicates that he will move away when the freeze is broken? Hands and fingers – what do they say about that person's feelings? What do all these details tell us about the person?

Note that at this stage no instructions have been given to the person involved other than to sit on the chair. He should be observed simply as a body, not a known person, nor an assumed character. The process is simply to analyse the messages received from a body occupying a defined space.

(b) A second chair can be added, and a second body. What is the relationship between the two? Do they know each other? Who arrived first? Are they aware of each other's presence? Have they been talking, or will they speak when the freeze is broken? Has the addition of a second person made any difference to how we view the first?

You can vary this exercise by giving each person to be observed a brief instruction, possibly based on emotion (as in an earlier exercise). It should not be seen as a guessing game – what is he trying to show? – but an opportunity to understand the importance of the physical in conveying information to an audience.

The time spent on these early exercises should be quite brief, and you will want to move on to work which takes them away from themselves and into assumed characters as soon as the information gained from the early work has been assimilated.

Status

Fundamental to the exploration and building of a character is awareness of status, how this is conveyed physically as well as verbally, and how it is recognised.

Status is the underlying aspect of all forms of human (and animal) behaviour. In any social interaction, the status of the participants has a major effect. In everyday life status can be immediately observable because of the function of the individual and the relationship to others – parent/child, teacher/pupil, employer/employee. It is also always present in less defined relationships, such as within a peer group. In both cases it can also be challenged, or shift more subtly, in a variety of circumstances. A challenge to authority can bring about change. In less clearly defined circumstances the shift can be more subtle, but is nonetheless observable.

In the imitation of reality which occurs in dramatic presentation, the actor's awareness of how status is defined, and the changes in status which can occur, is a major factor in the truth of presentation. For young people who are exploring the world and their roles within it, this knowledge is of immense value in their learning process.

The following basic status exercises are designed to demonstrate and explore how status can be conveyed and recognised.

1. Split the group into two and label each half A or B. Instruct them to walk freely around the space, making no eye or physical contact to begin with. Once the movement is established ask them to make eye contact with everyone they meet. Then instruct the As to make and hold momentarily a firm eye contact with everyone they meet, while the Bs drop their glance as soon as it is engaged. Run this for a short time, then swap over.

    When the exercise is finished, discuss the effect. How did it affect them to hold contact, or to drop it? Did they feel different, or move in a different way? If time allows, repeat the exercise with a few people withdrawn to observe it. What impressions did they receive? Did the group 'feel' different when there was no contact at all? When all made contact? When the group was split into different categories?

2. In pairs facing each other across the length of the room, instruct them to choose privately whether to be high or low status (i.e. holding or breaking eye contact). They then walk towards each other as if on a narrow, crowded pavement. As they meet and pass, their behaviour will differ according to the status they have chosen. Both may be of the same status, or they may differ. Again, repeat the exercise with observers, and discuss what they saw.

Both of these exercises provide a simple demonstration of status and how it is reflected and conveyed in physical behaviour in a very basic way. The following exercise is an exaggeration of status behaviour; it is verbal, and much more rowdy.

3. The group stands in a line, places chosen at random, with the person at one end facing in towards the line, the others facing him. He assumes a high status role, and status diminishes

along the line, each person being slightly higher than the next one. The first person asks a question or makes a demand requiring immediate response from the next in line, who kneels when spoken to (e.g. 'Where's the report I asked for this morning?'). Number two then stands and relays the message to number three, who also kneels, and so on down the line. The message can be reinforced or embroidered by each person at will. As the message is passing along, number one can repeat and reinforce his question, and this is also passed down. The last person in the line, who is of lowest status, can either 'produce the report' or provide abject excuses, which are then passed back up the line to number one. Again, the standing/kneeling rule obtains, with each person holding on to his original status.

If the exercise is repeated, ensure that people change places in the line beforehand. It is a noisy and enjoyable exercise, but within what may appear to be somewhat chaotic behaviour, an awareness and demonstration of the more subtle distinctions in rank, and how these effect behaviour, may emerge.

4.   This is another of the many variations on the park bench exercise, and enables a closer exploration of physical status signals. One person sits on the bench, having decided his status, and holds his position. (It is an advantage if the bench is not too long). He is joined by a second person, who can choose to play the same or contrasting status, which can be indicated by initial eye contact. The exercise is non-verbal, but once the second person sits down movement is allowed. A third person joins them, who has been instructed to choose a status which contrasts with the other two. If they are both high he plays low, or vice versa. If they are of different status he can choose to play much lower or much higher.

Allow the physical interaction to run for a short while. Then discuss what was observed. Were the differences in status clearly recognisable? By what signs? How did the arrival of the second and third person affect the behaviour of the others? With a more experienced group (and perhaps a longer bench!) you can instruct more people to join in, always offering a status which is slightly different to those already there.

These exercises can be used at many stages in the work of the group. They can be particularly useful when working on a play, whether scripted or devised, in which case the exercises are carried out in character.

Most of the preceding exercises are non-verbal, and when you wish to develop status work further you will need to incorporate some verbal work. This can be done in short improvised scenes, working with pairs or larger groups. In some cases status can be built in, in others it only becomes apparent by the behaviour exhibited.

5. Using a variety of scenarios, instruct them to choose status in advance along the continuum from very high – high – middle – low – very low, and to be sensitive to the signals sent out by the other participants in the scene, pitching their behaviour appropriately.

   There is a large range of possible scenarios, but the situations suggested for improvisation should not be too complex, and can work best if they are quite tightly focused The following can be used for pair work:

   - complaint (or purchase) in shop;
   - job interview;
   - police interview of suspect;
   - teacher/pupil encounter;
   - parent/child encounter;
   - householder/dustman;
   - farmer/trespasser;
   - doctor/patient;
   - passenger/ticket clerk.

   For larger groups:

   - dinner party, or other social gathering;
   - group stuck in lift;
   - outdoor expedition encountering some hazard;
   - group of people in pub/disco;
   - late night 'bus queue;
   - airport delay.

   These can be played either as spontaneous or prepared improvisations. The pair work is easier to do spontaneously than the group work, but experienced groups can usually manage this.

6. An extension of the above exercise allows for a reversal of role within the scene. That is, the apparently low status participant gradually becomes more dominant, while the other yields. To

start with, this is easier to handle in pair work, but, again, it is possible to do with larger groups. In this case, you may wish to start with clearly defined status, such as store detective/ shoplifter, or you may wish to start from a less obvious standpoint, such as two people meeting in a social environment, whose opening remarks and behaviour define their initial respective status.

When this exercise is performed and observed, useful areas of discussion can be centred on the point at which status began to shift, how easily it was yielded, the physical as well as the verbal indications of change.

7. The *master/servant* game described in Chapter 2 has an obvious place in work on status. There are many variations to the game, some of which include a challenge to status. One of these could be labelled 'the wily servant', which has a long theatrical history. Best played in pairs, the master accuses the servant of various faults and gives him orders, all of which are evaded by the quick-witted servant. For example:-

> 'Why haven't you brought my hot chocolate?'
> 'Because I'm waiting for the grocer to deliver the different brand your honour ordered.'
> 'Why haven't you brought my newspaper?'
> 'I wished to spare you the bad financial news.'
> 'Bring me my new suit.'
> 'I am afraid I am unable to.'
> 'Why, have you sold it?'
> 'Certainly not. I had to send it back because the quality of workmanship was not good enough for your honour.'
> 'What have you done with the money I gave you to pay for it?'
> 'I used it to put a bet on a horse.'
> 'Did it win?'
> 'No, it was the one you told me was a cert.' – and so on.

The master can 'kill' the servant and replace him with another, or exact punishment by hitting him with a rolled-up newspaper. For instance, if the answer to the first question above had been 'I thought it was time you went on a diet' that may have deserved a rebuke. However, the master could have ignored it to see how it would end. For example:-

> 'I thought it was time you went on a diet.'
> 'Why?'

'Because your honour's health and well-being are so important to me.' or 'Because you're too fat'—instant death or dismissal!

This exercise does require quick wits and an understanding of the conventions which govern it, and it is probably best to save it until the group has some experience.

A simple use of the master/servant game is to play it with a large group, with the variation that the master confers status on each participant at the beginning of the game, the simplest being a line in rank order. At the end of the game the master again puts them in line, according to how well they carried out their duties.

This is very much a game, rather than a skills-learning exercise, but it is relevant and useful when work is being done on the concept of status.

Intensive character creation

Intensive character creation is appropriate at many stages in a group's work. It has an obvious function in preparation for the production of a play, whether scripted or devised. Indeed, material for devised work can have its starting place in the creation of a group of characters, who will need to be well understood if an extensive work is to be done with them.

To create, explore and work within a different persona involves great demands of concentration and commitment, and you will have to judge when the group is ready for this. It must be done seriously and honestly, and every member of the group must recognise and respect what is being done by each individual. Initially, there may be a temptation to go for stereotypes, but even when these are offered it is possible to develop them beyond the two-dimensional by a sensitive and carefully judged response to the material which is offered.

The time spent exploring the created characters can vary. It may be appropriate to use this work just in one session, to give a taste of what can be achieved, but you may wish to carry this work over a number of sessions to allow a full development of what has been created and offered.

When you plan to lead a session on character creation, the warm-up and preliminary work should be chosen to provide an atmosphere of concentration, building up high mental energy

levels, rather than purely physical. It is more difficult to build up
the necessary concentration levels after a rowdy opening to the
sessions, and if this has happened a carefully chosen linking game
or exercise should provide the right atmosphere. Equally, if there
are likely to be intrusive external distractions, it is best to leave this
work for a time when a quieter environment can be assured.

The following exercise is one which concentrates fundamentally
on the individual engaging in an act of creation. How you run it,
and the instructions and guidance which you give, is a matter of
individual choice. The following is offered as a model whose
components can be varied according to your needs.

Everyone is isolated in his own space, sitting or lying, with eyes
closed. You may wish to talk through some basic relaxation as an
opening. They should mentally cut out all external sounds except
for your voice, and all awareness of the others in the room. You
then talk them through:-

> 'You are waiting for something or someone – a 'bus? a
> friend? for the rain to stop? – Who or what is it? Picture
> what you are waiting for. Where are you? Are you indoors
> or outdoors? What can you see? Are you cold or hot? What
> is under your feet? – Create your own environment at this
> moment. What time of day is it? What season of the year?
>
> Who are you? What is your name? How old are you?
> Where do you live? in a house? in a flat? a tent? a caravan?
> a squat? in the open air? in a town or in the country? –
> Create your own place, see what is in it. Do you like it?
> Have you chosen it for yourself? What does it smell like?
> What does it feel like? What is the first thing you see when
> you open your eyes in the morning? Do you live alone, or
> with other people? Who are they? Do you like them?
> Would you prefer to live somewhere else?
>
> Think back over what you have discovered about
> yourself so far and check that it all fits together.
>
> Do you work? What kind of work do you do? How do
> you spend your days? Do you have a lot to do with other
> people, or are you a solitary person? What are your
> personal tastes in food? music? clothes? life-style? What
> amibitions do you have? Are you contented with your life?
> Would you like to change it in any way?
>
> Are there things in your past that you are proud of, or
> ashamed of? What kind of background do you have? Do
> you have a family? Are you responsible for anyone else?

'How do you feel about them? – Picture the people who are closest to you, the people you like, the people you dislike. What do you look like? What do you wear? How do you move? Are you content with your own body? Do you feel happy in a crowd, or do you prefer to be on your own? Think back over what you have discovered about yourself. This is the person who is waiting for something or someone. Does it all fit together? If you need to change any of the details, do so now. When you open your eyes you will be the person you have created, and must try to remain that person until I tell you to change.'

The next stage has to be handled carefully, as you bring them back from their concentration on creating a new persona into surroundings that are familiar to them, but may have no place in the life of their 'character'. Tell them to open their eyes when they feel ready, to stretch and move, then to get up and explore the room on their own, in character.

When they have done this, you can move on to a number of possible developments, depending on the size and nature of the group, the time you have left in the session, and what you are planning to do with the work. The following are possible alternative strategies for the first stage.

● Ask them to sit down, choosing places appropriate to their characters. Ask each in turn his name, and for a few brief details, such as where and for whom each was waiting. Always address them by the names they have chosen, and make the tone and nature of your questions appropriate to what you learn about them.

● Ask them to form a status line.

● Place them in pairs, and ask them to find out as much as they can about each other, both remaining in character for the discussion and the reporting back. They then report back to the group the most important things they have discovered.

● Provide a small acting area with few stage properties, and ask each in turn to use the area to demonstrate something about themselves. This can be as simple as putting on shoes, coming in from work, watching television.

● Place a small group in an everyday situation, such as a 'bus queue, supermarket, station, and encourage improvised interaction.

● Instruct one person to drop his character for the purpose of the exercise (or take the interviewing role yourself) and interview some of the group as witnesses, for example to an accident, eliciting full details of name, age, occupation, and so on.

● Choose some simple exercises and games, and have them played in character.

Inevitably, during the session some characters will be dropped from time to time. This is natural and healthy. But if the preparation and building of the characters has been thorough, they should be able to regain them. It is important, however, to close this work as carefully as you instigated it, leaving enough time at the end of a session to reverse the process. Again, allow them to relax with closed eyes, and talk them back into their own characters. This need not take as long as does the building of the fictitious characters, but it balances and rounds off the work, and for some people, who work intensely on such exercises, it is essential.

Exploring and developing a created character

You may wish to extend the work on character, either within a long workshop or over more than one session. If there has been a break in the work, give them time and talk them through the re-creation of the characters, but more briefly than in the original exercise. They should be quite familiar with them by now. If anyone does not feel comfortable with his creation, allow him time to build a new one which he can test in subsequent work.

The following exercises provide opportunities for further exploration and development. They can stand on their own, purely as a self-contained discipline, or can be relevant to the rehearsal of a play.

Defining the character in other terms
The group walks around the room individually, in character. They can meet and greet each other. Then they come into a circle. Each in turn is asked to define his character as something different, such as

a month of the year, a time of day, a type of animal, a food, a country, and so on. Take this fairly slowly, building up the information gradually, using one category at a time. Let them walk around with each piece of extra information in mind before they assimilate the next one.

When they are all familiar with each other's characters, you can repeat this, asking them to provide the definitions for each other, and discussing any disagreements.

Finding the character's voice

This is not designed to teach them to mimic regional or social accents, rather to find a new pattern of speech, and possibly pitch, appropriate to their characters.

(a)   Ask them to walk freely round the room, and, when it seems appropriate, ask them to vocalise as they walk, something as simple as counting, saying the days of the week, the months of the year.

(b)   Put them in pairs and go through the 'talking in numbers' exercise, giving them a simple scenario, such as asking directions, meeting socially.

(c)   Choose a nursery rhyme, or any short piece of verse they all know. In pairs, say it to each other a line at a time, in character, in a variety of tones, such as angrily, persuasively, happily, and so on.

Exploring the character's status

By this time, there will have been a good deal of interaction between the characters, and they are likely to have made some adjustments to their ideas of relative status.

(a)   Repeat the status line, and see if it varies in any way from the first version.

(b)   Do the park bench exercise described earlier in this chapter, aiming for a flow of characters moving in and replacing each other.

(c)   Set up an 'information desk', such as at a railway station or tourist information office, and have them approach it to ask for information singly or in groups.

Throughout all these exercises, you will find it useful to let members of the group observe and discuss what they see with those who are doing the exercises. This helps each person find out more about his characterisation, and refine the truth of his portrayal.

Hot Seat

This exercise is most useful when preparing for a play, but can be used if you, and the group, wish to take the characters further at any stage in your work.

Everyone drops his character except for the nominated person. It can be done with the characters held (especially if you are working with a small, experienced group), but they usually disappear during the process, so it is best to get rid of them at the start.

The chosen person sits facing the group who, always addressing him by name, ask questions about his life, background, wishes, attitudes, emotions. Encourage them to follow a particular line of questioning, rather than jumping from one area to another. The aim is to help the person find out more about himself. The questions may move into areas which have not been considered before but if the person can remain successfully in character the answers will provide more information, and a deeper insight into the person he has created.

If you have a large group, it is probably too time-consuming to run this exercise with everyone questioned in turn, but even doing it with a few gives them a taste of what is possible in fully developing a created character.

There is an alternative method of character creation which takes into account the time factor. Using small groups, a character is invented, with about a dozen salient features of his life and personality put in place. One person is selected in each group to take on this role, is given a short time to assimilate the given details, and is then 'hot-seated' to explore his or her character.

This approach has some advantages, especially if you want the work to be contained within one session. Though everyone does not take on a character, everyone has an input, both in suggesting details about the character and in asking questions. It is less intensive and can be used as a one-off exercise to demonstrate how the hot-seating method works. If you want to move on to work in which everyone plays in character, however, the more intensive and individual approach is more apppropriate.

By this stage, having run a selection of suggested exercises, you should have a group of well-defined and understood created characters. This can stand in its own right, but you may wish to use them for further work, in improvisation and possibly devising for a production. The following are suggestions for improvisation scenarios.

1.   **In pairs**, with one dropping character,
     ● a television, radio or newspaper interview;
     ● interview of a suspect in a criminal investigation;
     ● a job interview.

2.   **In larger groups**
     ● an airport lounge or railway station;
     ● a hospital or doctor's waiting room;
     ● candidates for a job waiting for interview;
     ● a public library;
     ● a party or other social gathering;
     ● a delay at a frontier post in a foreign country.

3.   **Group work**, in which it may be necessary for some to drop their characters and play other roles.
     ● an over-confident or high status character out of work, in a job centre;
     ● a lowstatus character, such as a single mother, wins a luxury holiday;
     ● a social climber confronted by the genuine upper class;
     ● a shy introvert hosting a celebrity visitor.

An additional technique which can be used when playing any of these scenarios is to freeze the action at an appropriate point, and for all or some of those involved to reveal, in character, their true thoughts and feelings.

Character and caricature

There is a line of continuum in the creation and playing of a created character, the two extremes of which are realism and caricature, with stereotype somewhere at the centre beween the two. The work described so far has concentrated on the creation of realistic characters.

Any character created could exist simply in terms of stereotype (tramp, businessman, fashion model, pop star, housewife) and by manifesting the external signals of this role could be easily recognisable. When more character development work has taken place, the deeper levels of reality begin to flesh out the stereotype, making the character believable as a person, rather than a two-dimensional symbol.

Caricature is at the other extreme. Concentrating mainly on the physical, it can be used deliberately for a variety of dramatic purposes. Some exciting work can be achieved using caricature, and also by mixing playing styles, with one person playing naturalistically against a selection of grotesques. It can also be useful to be able to pitch the playing at different points between the natural and the totally exaggerated.

If you wish to set up work of this kind, it is always possible to base it on the stock commedia del' arte types, such as the cock, the gross, the naïf, the old man. Interesting work can be achieved using this traditional form, but a wider range of 'types' (which may be closely akin to those of commedia) can also be created using this freer method.

The group walks freely and naturally around the space. Once the movement has become flowing and concentration achieved, instruct them to focus on one other member of the group, always keeping in visual contact but without following closely. Each person should observe every physical feature of his chosen person, such as carriage of head, how the arms move, the length of stride, how the feet touch the floor. They should start to copy what they see, to attempt to become that other person as they walk.

The next instruction is to choose one physical feature which manifests itself in movement, and begin to exaggerate it. This exaggeration is then increased as far as possible into the realm of the grotesque. Then the new body shape is given a voice, a sound which is appropriate to its physical form.

By this time you should have an animated group of complete grotesques, and can round off the exercise there, with the instruction to come back gradually to their own normal shapes, but to remember the ones they assumed. Or the work can be taken in other directions, such as

- meeting and greeting others in the group;
- slowing down, and speeding up the movement;
- taking the caricature halfway back to the normal, and then

running the exaggeration backwards and forwards by degrees along the realism/caricature continuum;
- making a tableau with a given title;
- giving them imaginary different surfaces to walk on, different environments to move through.

Concentration on one physical characteristic to exaggerate brings with it a clarity in this work. The rest of the body should adapt itself naturally to the new shape it is adopting. It is also easy to remember and re-create as necessary. If they are only instructed to take on a new, distorted shape, the result can be an unfocused muddle, static, and difficult to move and use.

This knowledge of how to create and work a caricature is something which can be incorporated in many activities. Having set it up, you may wish to explore and develop it in other exercises.

- Set up a 'park bench' exercise, choosing an appropriate one of its many variations.

- Carry out the screen exercise, in which two or three players move around a screen in a random fashion, interacting, with the aim of surprising their audience.

- Give a theme for improvisation, or a location, for three or four characters. It can be useful here to provide them with stereotypes to play, such as public schoolboy, businessman, town councillor, vicar, teenybopper, busybody, headmaster, football hooligan. Ask them to work on a short prepared improvisation, to be played three times, the first time straight, the second with slight exaggeration, the third as total caricature, using body shapes they have created previously. Another approach to this exercise is to mix the playing styles within the scene. This is best done once all the possibilities of exaggerated playing have been explored.

Other possibilities are to use many of the preliminary and improvisation games and exercises while maintaining the physical caricature.

A major benefit of this work is that it enables them to recognise when they are playing with the kind of exaggeration which can result in caricature, and only to do so when it is dramatically appropriate. When it is done strongly and with conviction, it can produce exciting results. Its concentration on the physical, and how this can be used to make a dramatic point, extends their range, and helps free them from reliance on speech as the dominant means of expression. Combining physical exaggeration with a limited script opens many new areas of playing techniques.

Bringing the character to the script

While much youth drama is based on improvisation, scripts have their place in the working process. To provide a group with opportunities to work on scripted material purely for the sake of the experience, rather than in preparation for a production, helps to demystify the written play. If a group has some experience of using the words of others and making them their own, their own improvised work can be enhanced as they will have worked on a wider range of material than they have created for themselves. If you intend to use a scripted play for production, their previous experience of working with such material will make it far easier to begin using the text efficiently.

Scripts do not have to be of a published play, though there is plenty of appropriate material which can be used. The group can write them for themselves, to be shared between them and used as needed. To begin with, discourage any attempt to provide a story line that needs elaboration, complex movement, or development. Ask them to work in pairs to write a sixteen- to twenty-line script, for two characters, with the instruction to make it as simple and non-specific as possible. You may find it helps to provide a couple of opening lines, such as 'I haven't seen you for some time'/'Well, I've been around.' The characters should be simply differentiated as A and B. The scripts are then exchanged, and time is given for them to be read over and discussed, and amended if necessary.

Each pair can then spend a while creating characters to use with the script, and then go on to present the resulting scene. Having played it through, they then exchange the lines, keeping their own characters, the person who used A's words now uses B's, and vice versa.

This work should be observed and discussed. Which way did the scene work best? What differences did it make when they changed over? What was the relative status of the characters? How did the meaning and emphasis shift? Was the relationship between the characters the same, or did it vary?

This exercise can also be done by the whole group using the

same short script, provided either by you or by a nominated pair. The success of a script will depend largely on how anonymous and non-specific it is. It should provide for a very wide range of approaches and playing styles, with the created characters given the freedom to find and express themselves convincingly.

You may wish to take the work further, depending on the interest shown and the reason why you are doing it. If so, the development should start by reinforcing the created characters, using some of the techniques described earlier. If the written script is sufficiently open-ended, the pairs of characters can also improvise the further development of the scene.

An example of a short script that has been used successfully for this work is provided in the last section of this book. Extracts from the work of known playwrights can also be chosen. The plays of Samuel Beckett and Harold Pinter (in particular his review sketches) can provide material for some valuable and interesting work sessions.

Finding the character in the script

The work to be described here is fairly advanced, and would be inappropriate for groups who have little experience, and whose members do not work together seriously on a regular basis. It needs a longer time than a single session if it is to be undertaken effectively. You are most likely to want to do it in preparation for the production of a play, but groups may wish to work on scripted material in workshop sessions quite intensively without any immediate end in view, and if they find the material they are using interesting, you may find that they will wish to continue to work on it over a number of sessions. It is important, however, to put it aside before interest begins to flag.

For this work, you will need to choose a complete text, so that everyone involved can discover what happens to each of the fictional characters, who they are, what are their relationships with each other. This can rarely be achieved by reading a single scene. You can, of course, provide the necessary information yourself, but this is really a second-best option. It is preferable to find a relatively short complete text, without too many characters, because at this stage the focus is on how those characters can be interpreted and presented, and there are benefits in having more than one member of the group working on a given character.

The first stage is to allow the whole group to become familiar with the material at the same time. This can be done by reading the play together, sitting in a circle, with each person reading a speech in turn. Don't give out parts. If the play is too long to allow for this in one session, split it into workable sections. You can also make any necessary cuts at this time. You can then work on a section at a time, varying the activities within the session. By the time you have read through the whole play, work done on it will be enhanced by their completed understanding.

When the reading of all or part of the play has taken place, hold a short general discussion about the material. What impressions have the characters made? How do they relate to each other? What are their motivations? What are their aims? Do they achieve them, and if so, how? Why do they fail?

This discussion needs to be handled with a view to the dramatic nature of the material. They are not going to have to write an essay on it, but to re-create it in theatrical terms.

Choose a short scene involving a few characters. Two or three are ideal. Split up the group and get them to work on it in small groupings, using the original text. When they have become familiar with the scene and the characters they are playing, ask them to put the text aside and re-play it, using their own words. At this stage, they will be working on a fairly superficial level, but they will be exploring the characters' behaviour, attitudes and relationships.

Now bring the group together as a whole, and run a few of the chosen scenes, both with the original text and the improvised one. It is best for more than one group to work on the same scene. Discuss the different interpretations.

Go back to smaller groups and, using the same scenes, try to discover further information about the characters, taking into account what is known about them from the rest of the play. What do other characters say about them? Does their behaviour conform to those views? What do they say about themselves? What is their relative status? Do they have any physical or verbal mannerisms? How do they stand, sit, walk? Play the scenes again, using the script, taking into account this new information.

Set up a small acting area, with blocks, or chairs and a table. Ask them to come into the space, in the character they have been working on, and occupy it, doing anything they wish, for a short time – no longer than a couple of minutes. They can speak if they wish to, using scripted or improvised words.

Bring the group together and ask them, in turn, to define the characters they have been working on in other terms, such as an animal, a country, weather, time of day. See whether a consensus develops but there are no wrong answers.

At this point you can change the composition of the small groups by swapping people round if you think it would be of benefit, but they can stay with the same people if they are working well and happily together. They should, however, be able to keep the characters they have been developing.

Choose another scene, and ask them to work on it using the script, and taking into account all the new information they have about the characters they have been working on. Let this work stand as experience in its own right, without further discussion.

Using the whole group, ask a number of individuals to drop the characters they have been playing in order to represent others. They should be identified clearly, so that everyone knows who they are. You can use labels with the characters' names on them. Each other person, in character, approaches them in turn, and states his relationship.

> 'You are Antigone, and you are my niece.'
> 'You are Haemon, and you are my son.'

Once the simple relationships have been established, encourage them to explore the more complex and abstract.

> 'You are Antigone, and you are my problem.'
> 'You are Haemon, and you are my sorrow.'

The whole process up to this point has been designed to allow individuals to gather as much information as they can to bring to their characterisations. How far you wish to take it, and how much development you feel necessary, will vary according to the needs and nature of the group. Even at this level, it is quite intensive work, and is probably best handled in short, concentrated sessions, interspersed with some other activities, especially games. You may find they become totally absorbed (especially if they become fascinated by the material you are using) but even then it is best to change the activity from time to time during the sessions and, most important, finish with something totally different and energy-releasing.

If you want to take it further this can be done by helping them to discover the characters' objectives, both within the scene and within the play. This aspect will certainly have been touched on already but it can be interesting to isolate and focus on it.

Take a short scene, and ask them to read through it first, and decide what each character is trying to achieve at that specific time. Ask them to play the scene keeping that objective in mind.

Bring the whole group together and have the scene played again for all to watch. Run it once, then ask for it to be played a second time. During the second run it can be stopped at any point, and the characters asked what they are thinking about, what they are trying to achieve, how successful they are being, who or what is assisting or thwarting them. Discuss together whether the characters have objectives outside the scope of the scene, and how the scene played fits into this overall plan. Play the scene again with this information in mind, and see whether it varies in any way.

By this time, the whole group should be quite familiar with many of the characters and several sections of the play. Any continuation of this work (short of a full production) will probably be giving a number of scenes or a section of the play to groups to work on for presentation to the rest of the group. You could, of course, have done this without any of the preparatory work described here, but for groups who are interested in this kind of work and take it seriously the practice of character exploration and development can be worthwhile and fulfilling.

The creation and exploration of fictional characters develops an awareness of the complexity of human behaviour. Its value in drama work is self-evident, but it has the additional benefit of enabling young people to understand more about themselves, and about the other, real, people they encounter every day.

Chapter 4

Playing to the public

The time will come when any group, whether working in a youth theatre or a school, is ready to stage a performance. While workshop sessions are the core and the foundation of their work, the sense of achievement which comes from using and demonstrating their skills is essential for the personal development of the members of the group, and their sense of joint achievement.

Preliminary planning for a school production

In the school situation, there may be the demands of the public examination for GCSE or advanced level classes, or a request to stage a public performance. Examination work should represent the culmination of the learning and experiences that they have been engaged in over quite a long period of time. In some ways, an examination is like an audition, a very strange and unfamiliar experience. To play for an audience of one, and a critical and assessing audience at that, puts an added pressure onto what is already a situation of some stress. Practice varies beween examining boards, but in some cases it is possible to have a small invited audience present alongside the examiner, which can alleviate this stress by providing a more normal playing situation. In either case, the group will be helped to give of its best if it has had the opportunity to present its work to an invited audience beforehand. The composition of this audience should be as normal as you can make it, not simply their peer group, but also interested teachers, parents and friends. Thus they will have the chance to try out their work before being faced with the artificial demands of the examination.

When faced with the 'school play', you may well have to include a larger number of participants, or a differing and varying age group. If so, aim if possible for a long run-in time, to enable the chosen cast to work together, using some of the games and exercises familiar to the core group. This will help to weld the group together, and get everyone used to your working methods. It will also establish a group identity. This preliminary work should be chosen to impart the kinds of skills necessary for the production you have in mind. The members of the group will find out each other's strengths and weaknesses, and learn to respect what each person is offering to the joint enterprise.

It is likely that a school production will be expected to draw on many of the arts-based activities which take place in the school, such as music, dance, the visual arts. Depending on the choice of production, this can be an opportunity to create an exciting and varied performance. The debit side is that there can be pressure on you to create a shop-window of school activities. The dance group must have an important place to show off their work, there must be an elaborate set for the art department to work on, and what about the school orchestra or music groups?

Skills of diplomacy come into play here if you are to get the message across of the interdependence of the various arts disciplines in the making of good theatre – which should be your aim. It is worthwhile to get everyone on the staff who wishes to be involved together at a very early stage. Discuss the intended production with them, your overall vision of its nature, and encourage them to make suggestions and to offer the work necessary in the areas in which they have expertise. A strong production team, meeting regularly in the planning stage and throughout rehearsals, should give you the back-up you need without overbalancing the overall concept.

The production team will be strengthened if it includes a representative number of school students, who can be given equal responsibility for certain production areas. They can assemble their own groups to take on specified areas of work, such as publicity, front of house, stage management and so on. The marketing of the production could be given as a project to a business studies group, set design to an art class, but in all cases their work on these separate elements should relate back to the relevant member of the production team. You may, in fact, wish to appoint someone as producer, to act as coordinator for all these activities, if you can find someone willing to take on the task. This will leave you free to concentrate on directing the production.

Without this kind of back-up, directing and mounting a large school production can present you with far too much work to do to achieve anything that satisfies either you, or the people taking part. School play audiences tend to be woefully uncritical – pack enough youngsters onto a stage and nearly everyone in the audience will see someone they know or are related to, and they are satisfied. But you won't be. The whole episode will be a frustrating experience, as you will know that at least some of the cast deserve, and could do, so much better.

If you are going to be virtually on your own in mounting a production, aim for something small in scale, with a group of actors you have worked with regularly, to whom you can give your creative energy undiminished by the pressures of a larger enterprise. There is no point in doing it if the experience is not a good one for everyone involved. After all, who is going to benefit? Primarily, it must be the young people themselves. Taking part in a public performance is demanding in terms of commitment and responsibility, and for those who have worked for some time on learning the skills necessary to produce theatre seriously, nothing is worse than being part of a cast-of-thousands show which is all surface and no depth. This undervalues theatre, and it undervalues those who make theatre, amateur or professional. To aim for quality is worthwhile in any endeavour, and especially when working with impressionable, creative young people.

Preliminary planning for a youth theatre production

Youth theatre is different from the school situation. You, and your group, should have much greater freedom in the choice of time, place, and nature of production. This freedom will have its own constraints, such as technical resources, availability of rehearsal space, playing venues, the age range of the group, and their ability to take on a rehearsal schedule which will make greater demands on them than a once-a-week meeting.

Your location, and the availability of public transport, is also a factor to be taken into account. Part-time work at weekends may conflict with rehearsals, and, with a mainly teenage group, the times running up to and including school examinations have to be avoided. This can be a major problem if your members are drawn from a wide area, as schools are often inconsistent in their time-tabling of 'mocks' and other internal examinations.

Having negotiated all these hurdles, and found a period of time in which it is feasible to mount a production, you may find that there are some members of the group who cannot make a commitment to a production, for any number of reasons. If the group has established itself strongly, and if the members have realised that youth theatre work is not primarily aimed at mounting plays, this should not be a problem. Make sure that those people who cannot take part know that they can come in when rehearsals are taking place (even though this can be a bit distracting at times) and that any help they can give is valued. Most importantly, they must feel that they will be welcomed back after the production to take part in workshop sessions. This is easy when the group has been together for some time. In the early stages the practices and ethos of the group are not so apparent, but when people do come back after a production, whether they have been in it or not, the group is a strong and cohesive one.

The youth theatre leader as director

At this stage, it is perhaps relevant to consider the position of the youth theatre leader. There has been debate within the youth theatre movement about the role of the leader/director, and most research indicates that young people work best and are happiest when they have clear direction from a skilled and sympathetic leader whom they trust.

The youth theatre leader needs to have many skills. To perform effectively under the year-round pressures of organisation, running workshops, negotiating with funding and other agencies, liaising with schools, parents and youth organisations, requires administrative and diplomatic abilities. When it comes to mounting a production, all of these factors come into play, with the additional task of becoming, for a defined period, a director.

In some youth theatre groups, a director for a production may emerge from the membership. This is only likely to happen, or to be successful, if the group is relatively stable with mature, older members who have amassed some experience. In this case, the leader's role will be supportive and enabling, acting as a consultant rather than directly involved in the creative process.

But in practice this is exceptional. Most youth theatre productions are directed by an adult, who is likely to be the regular youth theatre leader. This does involve a subtle shift in role and relationships. A director is not a dictator, but however much democratic consultation and discussion take place within the group during the production process, however much the members of the group (collectively and individually) contribute to the creative process, it is the director who must make the final decisions.

A youth theatre director differs from a director in the professional theatre in one important aspect. He is not working with professionally trained actors. The young people involved are likely to have a range of skills which they have acquired during the on-going workshop process; they are also likely to have innate talents, but these are still relatively raw and unrefined. To direct young people successfully demands sensitivity and sympathy, the ability to recognise what they can do well and build on that, knowing what more they need and helping them to acquire those skills and the confidence to use them. This requires patience, intuition, a sense of humour, as well as a knowledge and understanding of what makes good theatre and the desire to exercise one's own creative skills within the medium of youth work.

The subtle shift from workshop leader to director is one which most youth theatre leaders undertake successfully. They can rely on the group to move forward with them into this new relationship, and the shared experience is usually an enriching one for everyone concerned.

Planning the rehearsal schedule

In the school situation, as well as that of youth theatre, it is important that the commitment to a production is clearly understood. A rehearsal schedule should be given at an early date, and kept to. If anyone knows in advance that certain dates or times are impossible, you should be told so that you can plan around them. Call times should be given. If you plan to rehearse a scene with two people in it for an hour at the beginning of a session, you don't want the whole group hanging around until you are ready to work them them. Call them an hour later.

Parents should not be forgotten. How you deal with them depends a lot on the nature of the group. For many youth theatre members, this activity is very much their private concern, but they need to be made to realise (tactfully) that it is much better for them if their parents know the work they have taken on, so that they do not plan a family holiday during production week. Good relationships with parents, who understand that they must not interfere, can be of enormous benefit to any youth theatre leader – or, indeed, teacher.

Choosing the play: devised or scripted?

The choice of play is all-important. You have two main options, devised work or scripted play. How to approach these alternatives is dealt with fully in the next two chapters, but it is appropriate to mention here some of the factors you may want to take into consideration.

Devised work is appropriate at different stages of a group's development. At an early stage, it can provide the opportunity for members to practise, refine and display the skills they have acquired, and to appreciate their relevance to theatre work. Later, more complex and demanding devised work can be undertaken. In both cases, experience in many kinds of improvisation is the key to a successful enterprise. And the group must be aware of the disciplines necessary to re-create improvised material and how to work on it to take it from the early stages and excitement of creation to performance pitch. The crafting of such material into a finished piece of theatre makes great demands on everyone involved, and as the work progresses it is important that everyone should be aware of the overall nature of the product they are working on, being prepared at times to sacrifice a favourite idea if it detracts from the impression to be made by the whole work, and to share and work on other people's ideas.

In the devising process, much material will be created, tested, and either accepted as relevant to the final product, or set aside as inappropriate. If the members of the group can accept that they are creating something together, and there is a degree of informed democracy in the selection of the material, this should not be too much of a problem, but you may find that a few egos may be slightly bruised in the process, and have to take the final responsibility for the choices. If the product is successful, this should cancel out any feelings of resentment. If it is flawed, you will have learned something from the experience. In either case, you will be able to build on it positively in the future.

When working towards a devised piece, the time-scale is all-important, and there is a different emphasis at different stages from work on a script. There needs to be a fairly long run-in time for the collection of material, and it can be perilous to try to curtail this. You will have to walk a very narrow path between giving sufficient time to this early process and the possibility of boredom setting in, as people feel that nothing is moving forward. When the selection has been made, the assembling of the material into a whole provides a fresh impetus to the work, before the (again quite lengthy) process of adaptation and refining of the improvised material to performance standard.

The great value of devised work is that it gives young people the opportunity to make their own statement. Their ideas and preoccupations are given value in a serious undertaking. They can speak to an audience of their peers and the older generation in their own language, they can question glib assumptions and facile stereotypes. They can provide an informed critique on the world which another generation has made for them to inhabit. They can suggest alternative structures and philosophies. When what they want to say is conveyed with theatrical skill and their natural energy, the result can be innovative and startling.

But the fresh and energetic approach of young people can be equally displayed when they are working on an existing script. The choice of play is crucial. It is commonly acknowledged that there is a dearth of good scripts for use by young people, and the few well-known ones by contemporary writers are probably relied on too heavily. In many cases, these are designed primarily for the large-cast school play, and rarely present much challenge to the individuals involved. This situation is showing some improvement, however. As the youth theatre movement grows, more published work of merit is emerging, some of it originating from devised work, some of it written for specific groups and now available more widely.

Moving away from plays written for young people, one has the basic choice between 'ancient and modern'. Plays are generally written to be performed by adult, trained actors, and those which are both modern and naturalistic need such players to deal with them convincingly. An adolescent girl playing a middle-aged woman, in, say, an Ayckbourn comedy is, at best, a brave imitation, at worst, grotesque. And the subject matter of such plays is usually irrelevant to young people, dealing as it often does with adult preoccupations and sexual games-playing.

Similarly, if one moves back in time to eighteenth-century drama or restoration comedy there are overwhelming problems, both of language and playing style, which few young people have either the capacity or the desire to cope with at this stage of their development. How about Shakespeare? A decision to stage one of his plays will depend on the nature and composition of the group you are working with. He wrote, of course, mainly for men, and his few female characters can present demands beyond the range of most young girls. The male/female ratio in most youth theatre groups (and many school drama groups) is heavily in favour of the female. The language can also present problems, as can the length and subject matter of the best-known plays, certainly most of the the tragedies. But there are some possibilities among both the comedies and the 'problem plays' for a choice of text which can be made accessible to young people, and admit cross-gender casting. And these plays do offer some marvellous possibilities for exciting and innovatory approaches.

Similarly, one can find classical Greek texts, and European medieval plays, which present actors and director with attractive challenges and timeless material, which can be re-created, as they always have been, in ways which are relevant to contemporary players and audiences.

But many other possibilities remain. The field of non-realistic twentieth-century drama is a large one, and there are many texts which provide eminently suitable material for young people to work on. And there is a great benefit for them in playing established work successfully. They feel that their skills are being valued in being given serious material to work on, and the process of making a recognised text their own increases their self-confidence and sense of personal worth, while enabling them to explore the ideas and language of major writers.

Undoubtedly, certain works by major playwrights are more suitable than others. For example, few would attempt Ibsen's *Ghosts* with a youth group, whereas *Peer Gynt* provides rich opportunities for an exciting production. Brecht's *The Caucasian Chalk Circle* is more suitable than, say, *Mother Courage*. Jarry's *Ubu* plays are within the range of many groups.

One possible restriction on the choice of a play by a relatively modern playwright is financial, as a performance licence must be obtained for a public performance, and in many cases the cost (especially for an unfunded group) can be prohibitive. This may rule out the plays of a whole range of modern, living writers, whose work is otherwise suitable for youth groups.

The following two chapters give a detailed account of approaches to production, first of devised work, then of a scripted play. The last stage of the process, immediately concerned with the final run-up to performance, is common to both, and is dealt with separately.

Chapter 5

Creating your own play

The concept of company-devised plays is one which is becoming more familiar in the professional theatre today, and even some adult amateur groups have successfully attempted this work. It is within the youth theatre movement that devised work has had its greatest growth. However, as the skills of improvisation become more central to actor training, those who wish to create plays have discovered that they can confidently ask actors to provide their own material, and theatre-in-education and community theatre companies increasingly take this approach. The work of Mike Leigh, in particular, gave an important impetus to this approach to play-making.

Improvisation can provide the raw material for a script, it can equally be taken through to final presentation without a final script being produced. Although the play needs to be carefully recorded in all the stages which make up its completed form, dialogue and action do not need to form a part of this record, and many, in practice, vary in detail from one performance to another.

The devised play is not an easy option to take, and cannot really be tackled successfully unless a group has a certain level of experience in improvisation which goes beyond immediate reaction to a given stimulus. There are inherent dangers, mainly those arising from showing an audience work which has not been properly prepared for public viewing. This is not to say that an enjoyable evening of short sketches, quickly prepared, cannot be produced, but it is only fair both to audience and performers to make it clear that it is just that.

The serious and valuable contribution to contemporary theatre which is being made by youth groups can be debased by the public presentation of work which is inferior because it is not founded on respect for the real demands of performance. While nobody expects young people to perform with the same skill as trained professional actors, an element of professionalism in their attitude to performance makes all the difference between a satisfying experience for themselves and their audience, and a self-indulgent exercise which is amateur in the worst sense of the word.

This approach to play-making makes great demands on the actors and the director. Once the safetynet of the script is removed, the level of concentration on the work has to be much higher than when there is the *aide mémoire* always on hand. But this concentration and total focus on what is being done brings compensatory advantages. There is a freedom to experiment, and extend the act of creation up to and within performances when a group has had the experience of working together intensively, and each member can rely on every other to react with confidence to the offers made within the context of the performance. There is an excitement which goes hand-in-hand with such risk-taking, which transmits itself to audiences who, perhaps subconsciously, feel themselves involved in the creation and development of something new at every performance.

It is in crafting a devised play that the major problems arise and important decisions have to be taken. Such work falls into two broad categories, one of which could be labelled **episodic**, the other **integrated**. The first term covers plays in which a central theme, or character, is displayed and examined in a variety of ways. There will be overall structure if the material has been crafted into a whole, but the lines of development of narrative will probably be neither complex nor sophisticated. An **integrated** devised play is one in which there is likely to be a much stronger story-line, and the material may be seen to follow a more conventional pattern.

Different skills of crafting are relied on in each case, but, broadly, it can be said that for an **episodic** play shaping, linking and balance are basic requirements and it is this style of production which can well be undertaken within the necessity for a script being written. An **integrated** play, on the other hand, is unlikely to be successful without a script, as the handling of the strands of the plot, character development and interaction, must rely on a predetermined structure.

In both cases, a longer run-in time for a production is necessary than for a pre-scripted play. The creation, gathering and selection of material cannot be rushed. There must be freedom to experiment, to develop new ideas as they emerge, and to make changes to accommodate them if they are valuable. If the play is to be scripted, time must be allowed for this to be done.

Who is to do this? It may be that you have someone in the group who is interested in play-writing, and this would be an excellent opportunity to give a young writer experience. If you have the skills and enjoy writing, you may wish to do it yourself, but it is an added task, and, if it is to be done successfully, it does take time. Either way, a break in the process is necessary. The group can take this time in learning new skills which may be relevant to the production, such as in dance or music, or you may be able to arrange the production schedule to take advantage of a natural break, such as the summer holidays, during which the script can be written.

The process of mounting a production of a devised play differs from the approach to a scripted play, certainly in the early stages, although if you are intending to make a script for this work the later stages of both are similar. The stages of the process fall into a broad pattern. The amount of time needed for each stage varies, and will depend on the nature of your group, the length and scale of the intended production, and the kind of material you are working with.

Preliminary work and choice of theme

The work you have already done on improvisation should provide a firm foundation, but it is worthwhile concentrating on different approaches to improvisation, experimenting with a variety of styles, as a run-in to the production period. Give the group the opportunity to flex their creative muscles: it's rather like tuning an instrument. Vary the exercises between spontaneous and developed improvisations.

You may find that this is an appropriate time to give them the challenge of a prolonged period of improvisation, with the built-in discipline of working virtually continuously over a stated time. A sponsored, non-stop improvisation session to last, say ten or twelve hours provides such a challenge, and can be used to raise a useful sum of money for the group. The time you can expect them to sustain this work will depend on their experience and confidence, and the size of the group. A small group of, say, up to ten people should not be asked to work continuously for more than about five or six hours, but a larger group should be able to last for much longer.

This activity should be regarded as something different from a marathon, and some work of good quality is likely to be done in the time allowed. I do not think that there is any benefit in doing it for longer than twelve hours. You will not raise more money, and simply to go on to prove a point devalues the work itself. Of course, not everyone is working every moment of the time, and to work well and be an enjoyable experience it needs careful planning.

This can be a very good way of building up the group's confidence and welding them into a strong working unit, giving them plenty of time to experiment with different styles and approaches.

Other preliminary sessions should concentrate on character work. A weakness in much devised work is that it can tend to concentrate exclusively on exploring a theme, and lacks the depth which should come from the performers' ability to create and sustain convincing characterisations of whatever protagonists are involved. The work is greatly strengthened if the performers can go beyond themselves, and beyond stereotypes, in their playing. Playing across the continuum from realism to caricature often finds a place in devised work, adding different textures and highlighting aspects of the theme being explored.

How do you decide on a theme? As the group is to create its own material, it must be fully involved in the decision from the start. There are a number of strategies you can use at this stage. One is to split into small groups with the task of tabling and exploring the issues which are most important to them, asking each group to come up with about three topics which they would like to explore dramatically. When the whole group shares its conclusions, you are likely to find a good deal of overlap, and several subjects which have thematic links, from which you can draw up a short list of topics to be worked on initially.

What the group wishes to explore will be affected by the members' ages, gender, social environment, current pressures, as well as the wider issues which they are aware of through personal experience and through media coverage. These topics are likely to fall into several broad categories – environmental issues, relationships, gender roles and expectations, morality, justice, bureaucracy, consumerism, and so on. All of these provide many possibilities for interesting work.

These are all worthwhile themes, and young people need to be given the chance to present them from their own viewpoint, entertaining and enlightening audiences. There are other possibilties, however, which may not immediately seem to present themes of such universal importance as those listed above, but which will be found to embrace many of them.

It may be possible to research an aspect of historical or contemporary life in your own neighbourhood, focusing perhaps on a particular character or event. If there is something of interest there, it is likely to involve at least some of the broader questions, as well as an isolated and individual story. An exploration of family life, contrasting and comparing the past with the present, firmly rooted in a known society and environment, can provide fascinating material, for which the research is part of the process, drawing on the skills of the members of the group in interviewing and dealing sympathetically with people of all ages and in different circumstances.

What you can do by way of such research will be defined by your particular circumstances. It may be limited to the families of the group's members, but you may also find it possible to liaise with an old people's home or day centre, which will allow a few people to come in and interview residents about their memories of the past. If these can be recorded on tape this will provide invaluable material for the devising process, giving examples of tone, patterns of speech and vocabulary, as well as the material you will be working on.

To explore attitudes across the generations, decide on a limited number of questions to be asked in exactly the same way to a selection of people – grandparents, parents, older and younger siblings, and others members of their peer group. Again, *how* the answers are given can be as important dramatically as *what* is said.

If it is possible for you to carry out this kind of research, even in a limited way, you will gather a rich hoard of material which will offer many possibilities for dramatic re-working. It will have enabled all members of the group to contribute in different ways, in interviewing, devising questions, and collating the results.

Activities can vary during this period. Some people may wish to start immediately on producing improvised work from the stimulus as it is being collected, creating the initial broad outlines from which future work can be refined. Others may wish to look beyond this personal material and find out something about the wider social and historical issues which provided the environment in which certain events occurred.

There are many other possibilities for collecting material for devised work. A starting point can be a picture, a poem, a song, a novel, a comic book. Tom Stoppard's play *Rosencrantz and Guildenstern are Dead* showed how dramatically rich the experiences of minor fictional characters – or any bystanders – can be when the focus is moved away from the principal protagonists and onto them. Taking any existing work, from a pop song, to a newspaper photograph, to a play or novel, you can explore the questions 'Who was he? What did he feel? What happened to him before – or next?'. You may find that you come to a blank wall, but even if you do, it might be possible to climb over, and see what is on the other side.

Throughout this preliminary stage, you will need to stimulate and encourage the process, establishing the structures which support it, recognising when it comes against a block and steering it into new and more positive directions. Always record what is valuable. Most importantly, you will need to be aware of the right moment to move on to the next stage.

The devising process

You have your theme and the material which supports it. The next stage is to select, refine, and begin the process of re-creating ideas and experiences to make a satisfying dramatic whole.

As far as it is possible, predetermine a time-scale for this stage of the work. Decisions will have to be made all along the way on what can be used, and what must be set aside. As a rough guide, four or five sessions (of approximately two hours) need to be devoted to this work. You are not bringing the material to performance standard at this stage, so any reworking of ideas should be directed towards exploring different ways of presenting them, rather than concentrating on detail. Make the research material available to the whole group, and encourage them to work in as many styles as they can handle. Give them the challenge of presenting a topic through mime or purely physical expression, with limited script, as story-telling, using caricature. Use dance and music as well wherever you have the opportunity.

Depending on the nature of the production and the material you are using, you may wish to provide, even at this early stage, a focus for the work. In broad terms, this can be character(s), theme, or situation. For example, if you have decided that the story of a particular person, or group of people, is to be the linking thread, you may wish to give the task of devising a variety of scenes in which he or they are central, exploring behaviour and reaction in different circumstances. If the theme is to be central, the work should focus on presentation of a variety of aspects of this theme, shown from differing perspectives.

To place situation at the centre of the work may seem an inversion of normal practice, but if, for instance, you are exploring how people behave under certain conditions – during wartime, in prison, at work – and the situation is firmly established at the centre of the work, the dramatic presentation of this situation is of equal importance to the presentation of human behaviour, and the work is greatly strengthened by this firm focus.

It is important that everyone should be able to see what everyone else is working on, so each session should be built around a time at which on-going work can be shared, even if it is only a scrap of an idea. Others may provide the suggestions which will be the impetus for moving it on, or a different angle from which to approach it.

The group is likely to have split into smaller sections for this work, and you may find that this gives rise to some difficulties which you will have to tackle. Even in a well-established group, there are patterns of friendship, leaders and outsiders, and the tensions which can arise can produce problems. The stronger and more confident tend naturally to coalesce, as they find it most satisfying to work with their equals, and they will often come up with the most exciting ideas. This can mean that other groups of less experienced and forthcoming people find it hard to produce work which initially bears comparison with that of the stronger groups, and may become discouraged and, at worst, feel under-valued. Equally, quieter people may find that their ideas are not being explored because of the people they are working with, who are more dominant but possibly less creative.

There is also what may be called the 'charisma syndrome'. It can happen that there is one dominant, usually very attractive, personality in the group, whose presence is thought to add value to the work of anyone he is working with, and a kind of competition arises to attract that person to the different groups. If the person concerned is mature and generous, this can in fact be an enlivening factor, but if (and it can happen) the reputation is based on very superficial talents, the work of the whole group becomes equally shallow and self-indulgent.

These situations demand careful management, and continual reinforcing of the whole-group identity. Even under the pressures of the devising period, it is worthwhile opening each session with a general activity. Warm-ups, trust games, spontaneous improvisation exercises such as *chain reaction* can all be used, and these also help to focus on the work which must be done in the session. Similarly, try to end the session with an energy-releasing game, or, if you are all tired, a quieter, more relaxing one.

As far as the smaller working groups are concerned, tact and diplomacy are required. The strong, confident people should be given the opportunity to spend at least part of the time working together. This is both fair to them and profitable to the overall enterprise. But there should be a fluidity about the groups, so that for the varying aspects of the work, people work in different groups. You will know from experience which mixes work and which do not, and while allowing some democracy in the choice of working partners, you should be prepared to mix and match whenever it is necessary.

Although your own creative role as director (assuming that you are not going to hand this over to a member of the group) comes into its own rather later in the process, you may well have ideas you want to experiment with in this devising stage. This may involve you in concentrating on a small group and sharing your ideas with them, trying out a variety of approaches. However, you may also want to explore dramatic possibilities which involve the whole group, and may feel it appropriate to do so at this stage. This again breaks down the jealously guarded fences which some people may have erected around their group and its work, and also helps to establish your role within the group, as an equal member when it comes to creative work.

By the end of this stage, you are likely to have created far more material than you need. Young people tend either to work very fast when they are stimulated into effort and flowing with ideas, or become completely blocked. Very few work at an even pace or can be predicted to produce a set amount. If you have been successful in providing the stimulus and the positive working environment, overcoming any personality problems and helping them when they are blocked, the result may be enough for a four-hour epic – which presumably is not what you want. However, as the work progresses it is essential to keep a record of everything which is produced, because although some of it will be set aside, even in these cases there may be a moment, or a germ of an idea, which you want to incorporate.

It is useful to have a system for this record. You may do it yourself, jotting down the essentials as you observe the work evolve, and then (if you are very organised) transferring this onto a more permanent record such as a card-index – or even computer program! Another method is to have a large sheet of paper pinned to the wall of your working space, ruled up into large boxes, and a supply of felt-tip pens, so that each group can make a brief record of its work. This need be no more elaborate than a note of the aspect of the theme they are working on, the style or approach they are taking, the names of those taking part, and other brief essential information. This format can be useful at a later stage, as eventually all the material available can be seen at a glance, and similarities, links and possible overlaps can be recorded on the sheet.

To script or not to script?

The essence of a devised production is the appearance of spontaneity. It is, of course, not spontaneous, rather the result of many hours of work – an illusion, like so much good theatre. The decision about whether the result, and the working process, will be facilitated by a script depends on many factors. A script need not inhibit spontaneity. It can provide the basis for new creativity, but conversely it can set the nature and tone of the production within over-rigid limits, and can be relied on too heavily as the production period progresses.

If you do decide to script, this decision must be taken at a fairly early stage, so that the time needed to prepare it can be built into the schedule. There are a number of options available. If the production is episodic, each group which has produced material can be given the task of writing the scripts for the episodes they have devised. The problem is that 'writing by committee' is rarely successful, and spontaneous dialogue which initially appeared fresh, inventive and realistic can become leaden when it is transmitted into words on paper. One person from each group could take on this work, but it can be a demanding task for the inexperienced, and the process of re-creating what was said or done when the group was working as a team is quite sophisticated, requiring a good memory for both detail and the whole, and a degree of objectivity.

You may have someone who wants to write, who can watch, record and produce a script for each episode. If you wish to take this course, it needs to be done with general agreement that this is the way things are going to be done, and the writer needs to spend a fair amount of time with each group, recording their work, discussing it with them, offering back the written script and then most probably, adapting it as the work progresses. Professional writers do work in this way with theatre companies: however, if you do have someone who wishes to attempt it, it is only fair to make sure that he recognises the complexity of the work, and the time and energy that it demands.

The same applies if you decide to script it yourself, and in both cases there must be an acceptance on both sides – the performers and the writer – that a degree of flexibility must be allowed in the handling of the final, agreed, material.

If the play is to be totally integrated, rather than episodic, something which is more along the lines of a 'conventional' play, incorporating plot, character development, working towards a resolution, the need for a script is greater. The framework of the plot needs to be firmly established, the behaviour, relationships and speech patterns of the protagonists must have coherence, and there must be a strong movement forward in the action.

It is not easy to devise a work of this kind with a large group. The overall framework must be in place at a very early stage, otherwise simultaneous working on different stages of plot and character development is almost impossible. One approach would be to introduce the theme of the play, workshop different aspects with the writer observing, and then send him away to produce a completed script which incorporates the ideas which he felt relevant from what he saw of the group's work. Thereafter, it could be produced as a scripted play. This approach is something of a compromise between devised and scripted work. It could be effective if all the elements for success were present, most important being a skilled writer.

What if you decide not to script? Is it possible to keep a grasp of what is being created, and carry it forward for further working from one session to the next? Strategies for recording work in progress have already been suggested, which are necessary whether or not you are going to script. With this record as an *aide-mémoire*, it is realistic to expect the people who created the work to remember most of the detail and the words they used sufficiently well to carry the work forward themselves. As they are speaking *their* words, they are more likely to be comfortable with what they are saying than with someone else's interpretation of them, and will therefore be able to remember them more easily. It is inevitable that they will be changed, radically or slightly, as they refine the original ideas for performance, and even in performance they will have the confidence of familiarity which underpins an appearance of spontaneity.

In this case, they need to be aware of certain disciplines. Each person is responsible for his own performance, but also for that of the group. An extra alertness is needed to ensure that no blocking occurs, especially if someone loses his way. Offers must be accepted, but no self-indulgence must creep in. Cue words and actions must be consistent. New material cannot easily be incorporated in performance – what is happening is as important as what is being said.

In the end, you may well decide on a compromise. Unless you are going for a fully integrated play, you are likely to have some groups who can develop their ideas happily without a script, others who decide to write a sketchy script and rely on it only to refresh their memories, while others may decide to script their ideas more fully. Like so many aspects of this work, it depends on the nature of the group, and your sensitivity to their needs, collectively and individually, will govern the decisions you make.

Use of related disciplines and technical assistance

The nature and style of the intended production will determine which of the related performance disciplines (music and dance) you wish to incorporate. It is very likely that you will have people with such skills within the group, and a devised production gives them an opportunity to use these relevantly within the framework of a theatrical event.

Responsibility for providing this input can be given to individuals and groups, but you must avoid the danger of their work being produced in isolation and taken to a stage where it does not integrate happily within the whole. The people in these groups may or may not wish to act: either way they need to be aware of the other work which is taking place, the tone and the theme of the whole production, so that what they do is a part of it, not standing alongside.

Music

With musicians in particular, try to encourage original work. If you need songs, get them to write ones which they and the whole cast can sing, preferably with both new music and new words. There can be the temptation to use standard or pop songs, and write new words for them, but totally original material is far more effective and convincing.

Dance

Dance is, per se, more likely to be original, but, again, if it can be done to new music it is doubly so. Dance should reflect and enhance the acted material. It can present new aspects of the theme. It can arise from action, and intensify it. It can provide commentary, maybe ironic, maybe contrasting.

Professional help

These are aspects of production for which you may wish to call on other professionals for assistance. Local community dance companies are often happy to work with youth groups, as are musicians, both teachers and freelance performers. They will need careful briefing and, as it is unlikely that they will be willing or able to attend every devising session or rehearsal, must be kept up to date with the development of the work, so that their skills in teaching and encouraging the original work can be fully used. People who are happy to accept the role as part of the team will be most useful to you, not those who wish to impose their own ideas, but those who can make a good contribution to work which they are not going to perform themselves. Most importantly, they need to respect young people and the ideas which they have chosen to work on.

You will need to monitor the development of this related work, ensuring that it keeps to a schedule which will allow it to be ready for whole-group working, or to be fitted into the framework at the necessary stages of production. There are many advantages in working with other professionals. They are going to be aware of rehearsal and performance discipline, and their creative input is supportive to you and the group. Young people learn a lot from working with them on a mutual project, and will respect the skills and disciplines which they are able to share with them.

It is worth mentioning here other aspects of the production for which you may wish to bring in expert help. **Set, costume, properties and lighting** are all essential to performance. What you will need will be determined by the nature of the production. Of course, you and the group can make choices, but, again, if you can call on professionals for advice, the group will benefit both in what they learn and experience, and from the final production standard they achieve.

Set

Unless you are going for complete naturalism, a simple, representative or abstract stage setting is easiest to construct and handle. Stage blocks and scaffolding can be used effectively in many different ways, and can provide you with a multi-level set. Colour is important, and should be appropriate to the mood of the production. Don't use gloss paint, as it lights badly. Gauzes and large swathes of material can be exciting, either permanently in place or used to make a dramatic effect. Some advice from a theatre designer can help you to choose appropriate materials and use them efficiently. Of course, you may opt for a bare stage (which has its advantages!), but whatever you decide on, think about how it is to be used by the performers, and avoid clutter.

Costume
Regarding costume, much youth drama tends to be set contemporaneously, and here you will rely on what the group can provide, but you may want to achieve a coherence in colour and style. Any kind of period or specialist costume, if you need it, is best hired, and local repertory theatres and many amateur dramatic companies have extensive hiring facilities. The former, at least, can also provide advice. If you are working in a school, you may be fortunate to have a skilled needlewoman in the home economics department who would like to supervise wardrobe. Again, the demands of the production and its nature must be paramount in determining what is provided as costume. Movement on stage cannot be inhibited by skin-tight, non-stretch materials, and high heels can be lethal.

Props
Stage properties can provide difficulties, because props-making is a skill of which few outside the professional theatre have any knowledge. Again, if you can get professional help for any specialised requirements, seize it. Otherwise, give some basic, sensible advice to whoever is to be responsible for finding and/or making properties. If there is to be physical work in the production, jewellery must be banned, or specially made from soft materials. Plastic glasses and plates are always safer than 'real' ones. If you need stage weapons these, again, should be carefully designed and made from non-injurious materials.

Lighting: Design, operation and safety
Lighting is another important area which needs early consideration. Here, the constraints are likely to be where you are playing and the resources available to you. Most schools have at least some stage lighting, but if it is not used regularly, or, even worse, you suspect that it has been misused, have it checked by a lighting expert before you use it. If you have nothing available you will have to hire, and it is worthwhile building a relationship with a company which provides stage lighting for the advice you can receive. Some local authorities have their own resource centres, and

will hire lighting and sound equipment at less than commercial rates. In all cases, make sure that anything you hire is in good working order, and that spare bulbs are provided.

Who is to design the lighting for the production, and who is to operate it? This depends on your circumstances, but if someone in the group wants to do it, make sure that he is given some proper training before a switch or a lantern is touched. Theatre lighting is a complex skill to learn, and can really only be taught by experts, but some amateurs have a reasonable grasp of the subject. If you can invoke the aid of a qualified theatre technician, do so: if not, find an amateur you trust to oversee what is done.

Remember that this is the most potentially physically dangerous aspect of the work you are doing. You will almost inevitably have to make compromises as far as lighting design is concerned, but with imagination much can be done with little, and you should allow sufficient time for experiment during the production schedule. But compromise should never be made with regard to safety, so ensure that any short cuts that are taken are not ones which could result in injury to people, or damage to property.

Sound
Sound is the allied aspect of the technical work, and, although this rarely involves physical risk, similar checks and advice are needed.

The importance of the backstage and technical work should never be forgotten, and you will probably find people in the group who are keen to concentrate on these. Their work should be given a high profile, and the more training you can provide for them the greater will be their satisfaction and enjoyment.

Creating the framework for performance

If you have decided to script the devised work, you can skip this stage of the process. However, if you are bringing together a great many ideas, thematically linked, you need to devise a framework or a context in which they can be presented.

It is basically a question of how to open, how to link, the appropriate sequences, and how to close. It may be a review style production, presenting a series of sketches, music, dance: but even this format can be used more positively if there is a structure in which the episodes are placed, rather than an unlinked sequence of dramatic happenings.

The framework must have relevance to the work it contains, and when it is successfully constructed it will enable smooth transitions from one episode to the next, one style of performance to another. It can also be used as a point of reference, it can provide commentary, and move the action forward. It can give the actors the opportunity to step in and out of the different roles they are playing without losing the impetus of performance. It can also be a device whereby the group is seen working as a unit, from which individuals may step from time to time to take part in the different stages of performance, and to which they return.

The nature and style of this framework will depend on the production in question, but the following are a few suggestions which may be adapted for different circumstances.

Theme
Exploration of the changes in lifestyle over a period of years in a small community, or between generations in a family.

Framework
- Open with group finding store of old newspapers/magazines/photographs.
- Discuss/react *as themselves*.
- Move on to presentation of prepared material, using flashbacks, returning to the group or individuals for comment/linking between episodes. The action can be chronological, or use contrasting episodes/attitudes. Characters can be paired.
- Return to group at the end for appropriate close.

Alternatives
- group of students doing local research
- multi-generation gamily reminiscing;
- use of music and 'Brechtian' commentator.

Theme
Environmental or social issue.

Framework
Use the concept of time-travel, forward and/or backwards. Either way, you can introduce the device of the innocent on-looker(s) caught up in and commenting on events. A similar idea is that of the 'wise alien'.

Alternatives
- A formal debate, in which the propositions and arguments are dramatised.
- A 'how did we get here?' situation, e.g. a group at crisis point examining the stages by which things got to where they are, and possibly looking towards changes/solutions.
- Again, music can be used for linking purposes but it really needs some verbal input as well to make the themes clear.

A challenging, but potentially very interesting, framework can be to use the rules and playing style of a familiar game. Television quiz games have been over-used by youth groups as the format for devised work, though they are always a new experience for some. But well-known board and card games can provide exciting dramatic frameworks, and can be exploited for their visual opportunities. *Monopoly* and *Snakes and Ladders* have obvious links with themes you may wish to explore, and there are others which could have similar associations. They should be chosen not just for the thematic associations, but also because they are familiar to the people who will make up your audience, so that the framework reinforces the dramatic material.

It is worthwhile finding your framework at a reasonably early stage in the devising process. This will enable you to develop it alongside the material which it contains, and time should be put aside to work on this. If it is too restrictive, scrap it and find an alternative. If it works well, you will find that it helps you to group certain sections, providing built-in contrasts and commentaries. And it will also be an aid in the selection process, which is your next stage.

First selection of material

You should by now have an overall concept of the nature of the production, its tone, and its format. You, and the group, will be aware from the progress of the work which ideas have been the most successful and the most relevant. You will find that there are some things which even their creators wish to abandon, and unless there are overwhelming reasons to keep them it is best to regard them as stillborn.

While you will want to exercise as much democracy as possible in selection (which at this stage will not be final), in the end you may find it necessary to exercise a little benevolent dictatorship as well, and the group is likely to respect your judgement if you have a good personal and working relationship with them. Your aim should be to end up with a 'long list', which may lengthen to accommodate new ideas, is likely to be very much shortened eventually, but which contains most of the material you feel is relevant to the work you are doing.

You should aim for as representative a selection as possible, not biased too much towards a particular style or the work of particular individuals. Look for dramatic contrasts, varying lengths of episodes. Are there any gaps which need filling, which will mean creating some new material? If you are using music and/or dance, how will what has been produced fit into the overall concept?

You may find that certain ideas are being repeated. Can you combine to make a satisfactory unit? If not, which are the strongest in theatrical terms?

Look at what you have in its relationship to the chosen framework. How can the episodes be arranged to the best effect? How can they be introduced, and commented on, if necessary?

As stated earlier, this choice can be democratic, but you may wish to approach it by asking the group to select some representatives to work with you in making the selection. However you approach it, everyone needs to know that the stage has been reached at which, except for absolute necessity, you are going to be working intensively from now onwards on refining the material which has been created rather than finding new ideas, and that you have the basic material for the production.

First mock-up

As a leader of a group of young people engaged in theatre work, your task goes beyond that of teacher and director, though it combines both of these. A fundamental aspect of your work is concerned with the emotions and expectations of your group, and you need to be alert to the varying moods of individuals, and of the group as a whole.

What has this to do with the first mock-up of a devised production? A great deal. By now you will have been working together for many weeks on collecting material, selecting, improvising, rejecting some ideas and concentrating on others. There will be a familiarity with the material which can mark the onset of boredom. This is one of the times at which you can find unexpected personality clashes, people who worked together happily in the past decide that they loathe each other,

and all the creative energies, including yours, are at a fairly low ebb.
This the time when something new needs to happen to provide the
impetus to get the group over this hump and give them renewed
enthusiam for the project.

There is something about the first run of the show, in what
approximates to its final format, which creates this new excitement.
It should be regarded as something of an occasion; there should be
a certain formality about it. The group should be given notice of
when it will take place, what time they are called for, what they
may need to bring in the way of properties and costume. The music
and dance groups should be prepared to perform what they have
been working on, even though their work, too, is unpolished.

You should by now have decided on the nature of the playing
area, and the kind of set or stage furniture you will be using. If you
are playing on the level, in the round, transverse or thrust, mark
out the playing space. Make a first decision on the position of exits
and entrances, though you may decide (depending on the nature of
the production) that the whole group will remain on stage
throughout. Have lighting available; mock-up a rough lighting
set so that they will be playing in a lit area.

All of these physical preparations can be devolved to members of
the group, and you may find at this stage that someone wants to be
stage manager, whose duties can start from this time.

As far as the material is concerned, take your 'long list' selection and
put it in an initial running order, taking into account who is involved
in which parts, so that you can balance both the nature of the material
and the players, making sure that people are not over-used at any
stage, and that they can have some breathing-space between episodes
of demanding work. Write up the running order and make it available
to everyone before the date of the first mock-up.

On the chosen day, bring the group together for a warm-up session,
and give them basic information about opening positions, cues,
entrances. Remind them that this is a run. It will move forward to its
conclusion without stopping except for dire emergencies, and all their
concentration must be on performing their work throughout the time
it takes. If the show will require it, you can build in a short interval, but
no other socialising should be taking place.

As the show runs, take notes. Not so much on performance, but
on what works, what doesn't, what needs to be moved, what may
be dropped. Are any staging problems apparent? Does everyone
know what he or she is doing? Are they in the right positions to
come on at the right time?

Time the show. This will give you a rough indication of how long the final version will be. If you are super-efficient (or, better still, have a non-acting assistant who can do it for you) time each section, which will help you make decisions when you come to re-arranging items.

At the end, you will find that the group is exhibiting a wide variety of reactions. Some may be elated, from just having got through it reasonably well. The more realistic, who tend to be the majority, will have a more sober reaction, recognising what worked well, and also how much work is needed before the show is in a fit state to be put before an audience.

Talk it through with them, finding out their reactions, what problems they had, what they enjoyed, what they didn't, and share your thoughts with them. This talk-through session needs to be positive in tone, with the object of setting up the final stage of work towards performance. Don't make it too long, but aim to get a few practicalities dealt with alongside the artistic assessment. Take notes of anything they say which will be crucial to your own forward planning.

By the end of the day, you should have helped the group rediscover enthusiasm for the project, and confidence that it can be carried through. By providing a performance environment in which the work can be tried out, you will have shown that it is taken seriously, and even if certain items are put on one side in the final selection process, they too will have been treated as valuable, and their creators reassured.

Final selection

After the first mock-up, you should have all you need to make the final selection. Though you will have seen it all before (many times!), seeing the material in the context of performance will put it in the perspective of the show as a whole. If there were two fairly similar ideas, you should have been able to see which works best. It may not, in fact, be the best developed, or performed, but it is the one that fits in.

Look in particular at how the material works in the context of the framework. What changes are needed to either to produce the best effect?

The most important artistic decision to be made is on the balance and range of material, and the tone which you are aiming to achieve. Organisation of the episodes within the framework is the key to this. Avoid having too many episodes which are similar in style close together. Balance the pace over the whole piece. What impression do you want to make in the opening moments? Do you want to sustain this mood, or to startle the audience with a contrast? Is all the material building towards some kind of statement? If so, is the statement clearly made? What impression do you want to end with?

Like all the other decisions, you can always make these with the help of the group, but it does not help them if the democratic process results in a muddled and unsatisfying product. This is one of the occasions on which you may have to take the responsibility of making choices for them, and it may be that some people will not be happy with your decisions. Such problems can be alleviated if you discuss fully your reasons for making certain choices. They should realise that if you are to direct the show, you must be reasonably happy with its content.

These decisions need to be made quickly after the first mock-up, because the stage of proper rehearsals must begin now.

Rehearsals

Depending on the state of the material for the show, your final rehearsal process can be fairly short, though intensive. Make sure that the group is aware of the new stage they are moving into, which has rather different demands to those of the earlier devising process.

Organisation is the key to sanity and success. By now, you will have fixed your performance dates and venue(s), so you can work back from them to establish the rehearsal schedule. There are other factors you will need to take into account, such as possible interruptions from holidays periods, school examinations, weekend jobs, and local transport facilities. If at all possible, try to put in some full-day sessions, probably at weekends or during a school holidays period. A whole day of intensive work is worth much more than three two-hour sessions.

Draw up a rehearsal schedule, and make sure everyone has a copy. If anyone knows that he cannot make a specific date, he should tell you well in advance. It's useful to have a list of dates pinned on a notice-board so that any absences can be written in. Make sure that you have everyone's phone number (or another method of contacting in an emergency) and that everyone has a way of contacting you.

In order that you can all make the best use of the time available, plan the rehearsal schedule in a way that allows you to work with particular groups and individuals at specified times, so that you do not have a large group waiting around with nothing to do. Giving call times as well as dates will clarify this. Your rehearsal schedule could look something like this.

date and times	call time	sections	cast
Tuesday 10/2	1900	3 and 5	Tom, Helen, Claire, Jon
1900 – 2100	2000	opening and links, first half	everyone
Saturday 14/2	1100	1	Tom, Andy, Jocelyn
1100 –1700	1100	2 (dance)	Rose, Anna, Helen, James, Matthew
	1330	4	Andy, Jo, Emma, Chris
	1430	run-through first half	everyone

and so on.

You are going to need a stage manager, and if you are lucky you may have the luxury of a couple of non-acting assistants who can share these duties. The rigid professional distinctions between backstage and technical staff which exist in theatre houses are irrelevant to the work you are doing. It is more a question of knowing what needs to be done, who wants to do it, and dividing up the work accordingly. The one distinct function is likely to be lighting apart from which one or two non-acting persons to take on backstage responsibilities during the final rehearsals and performances is usually enough. A small team, if you have one, can be given the responsibility of organising the work between them.

If you aim towards a complete run-through halfway through the rehearsal period you will have a good idea about how the production is shaping up, and the group will also be able to assess their own work and what more is needed.

As you rehearse, keep reminding them that they are going to be playing to an audience, and that in particular they must work seriously on diction and delivery of their words. This can be a big hurdle for some young people, as most of the workshop sessions which they are used to require them only to perform for very small numbers of their peers, and the focus tends to be more inward.

Whatever shape of playing area you are using, encourage them to visualise the audience. Rehearsal techniques which may help include getting them to alternate between shouting their words, and whispering them audibly, playing their lines *very* slowly, saying their words to each other from opposite corners of the room.

If you are using music, make sure that some parts of rehearsals are set aside for concentration on this element of performance, so that the musicians, actors and (if you have them as well) dancers are all in tune with each other's needs, and that any group work can be practised to the point of confidence.

During this time, final work on the set, costume and lighting will be taking place. This should also be working to a schedule. It can be disastrous if your set crew decides to re-paint everything just before you want to do a run-through. The technical planning is as important as rehearsing the actors, and you will need to set up lines of communciation and liaison with every aspect of the production. You can use your stage manager to coordinate this.

Final shaping and checks

As you near the end of the rehearsal period, take some time to stand back, together, and make a critical assessment of what you are going to put before the public.

Does the show communicate? Does it entertain – in the broadest sense? Do all the elements combine successfully? Have they been properly balanced?

It is too late to make any radical changes, but even at this stage it is possible to make some shifts and alterations in sequence and emphasis, if you feel they are needed.

This is the time, too, to re-emphasise and practise some basic skills; things as simple as holding a freeze, moving in slow-motion, using the playing area efficiently, awareness of focus, moving stage furniture smoothly and quietly.

Hold a meeting with the backstage crew, and the technicians, and everyone else who has been involved on the production side. Give them a chance to ask any questions they may have, and ensure that everything in their departments is ready for take-off.

A check list of final tasks is given in the last chapter, which may help to take the work smoothly from rehearsal to performance.

Chapter 6

Re-creating a scripted play

Given the right play and the right approach, work on an existing script can be as exciting and original as devised work. The choice of play has to be made within the constraints of the nature of the group and the resources available – finance, manpower, technical, space, time. But many of the problems which these factors produce can be minimised by some creative thinking, and if you find a play which you are all enthusiastic about you are likely to find the right solutions.

Certain considerations have to be taken into account. The playscript is a working tool, and the history of the theatre shows that the interpretation and presentation of plays change with fashion, current theory, and every director and cast which work on a particular text. The best results come from a partnership between the work of the writer and those who re-create his work for presentation to an audience. This involves a degree of respect for the original work, which does not allow the themes and the overall nature of the play to be distorted or destroyed in the service of a particular theory held by those who are performing it. If a play has to be altered so much in its presentation that its nature is completely changed, the question must arise why it was chosen in the first place.

This can be a temptation when working with young people – to seize on those elements of the text which may initially appear attractive to them, and thus appear easier to deal with, to the detriment of the whole. Shakespeare in particular provides such traps. Productions of *Macbeth* in which the weird sisters dominate, and both the central relationship and the balance between good and evil are pushed to the sidelines; *Romeo and Juliet* reduced to a series of street brawls; *A Midsummer Night's Dream* with the mechanicals and the Pyramus and Thisbe episode becoming the major source of energy in the production.

But it is quite possible to deal with a play by Shakespeare, or any other playwright, in a way which fulfils the need to make it accessible to young players, and attractive to an audience, whilst being honest about the nature and intention of the original. Given a well-considered approach to the play, the (sometimes drastic) cuts which may be necessary will be balanced throughout the text, and can often clarify the lines of development of themes and character. The shape and pace of the original need not be distorted even if you wish to place greater emphasis on one theme rather than another, providing some degree of balance is retained.

One of the great advantages of working with a young cast is, paradoxically, their relative ignorance of theatrical conventions. They will not approach a text, even a well-known one, with minds full of the clutter of remembered past productions. Almost anything becomes possible with regard to staging and style of production. They seldom wish for the impedimenta of realistic sets, properties and 'authentic' costumes, being more interested in the physical performance of the play. They will be interested in the general style of the production, though, as it will have a direct effect on their playing, and discussion about how the production will look, staging requirements, the range of colours to be used for any set and costumes, forms part of the re-creation process.

Early decisions may be revised later in the process, but if the keynote to the production is set at an early stage, the whole process will be facilitated by the links you have established between the text, the visual impact of the production, and the style of playing.

The process of selecting, adapting and rehearsing a scripted play should be designed to allow for the maximum contribution by the group, as individuals and as a whole. Every play has its own demands, just as every group has its own strengths and weaknesses, so when discussing possible approaches, generalisation is inevitable. However, you may find it useful to explore some of the methods suggested here, and try out those which are appropriate to your purposes. The suggestions follow through the course of the rehearsal process, and there are, inevitably, some similarities and overlaps with the approach to devised work. These are repeated here (though not necessarily in the same words) rather than cross-referenced, for ease of reading.

Choice of play

In Chapter 4, I discussed some factors which have to be considered in choosing a play, and it is valid to reiterate and expand on a few of these here.

Are you considering a play which has been written for performance by young people? If so, discuss it with the group, give some of them copies to read and come back with their assessments. Is the material timeless, spot-on contemporary, or slightly dated? If the latter, can it be adjusted to bring it up to date? Are they interested in the theme? Are the characters believable? How well has it been written? Does it portray young people honestly and sympathetically, or does it patronise, or deal in stereotypes?

What about a 'classic' play? The challenge of re-creating a major text for performance is a tough one, but one which appeals to many young people. It shows that they are being taken seriously, and their abilities are not underestimated. But this should really only be attempted if they are enthusiastic about it, and you feel confident that they will be able to handle it. Again, consultation with the whole group as well as with individuals will help in deciding whether this is the course you wish to take.

The contemporary adult theatre repertoire (from, say, 1960 onwards) does not really have a great deal to offer which is suitable for youth groups, except for those at the top end of the age range. Suitable for performance, that is. Short plays, or extracts from full-length ones, can provide excellent workshop material, and it is possible that you may have worked on such a text and can see ways in which it could be presented for public performance. If you have confidence in the group's ability to handle it, give them the chance to take it through a production. They will learn a lot in doing so.

The assumption that underlies this discussion is that you are not looking for one of the never-mind-the-quality-look-at-the-size-of-the-cast plays which have become depressingly popular for school productions nowadays. These offer very little to anyone who has any real interest in theatre work, or faith in the creative abilities of young people. They generally rely on a handful of 'starring' parts backed by a nameless throng of chorus. There has obviously been a slot into which they have fitted, as they can make maximum use of available personnel. Parents are satisfied and the local paper will print a photograph with flattering comment, but they offer few opportunities for serious work and undervalue the abilities of those taking part.

Another assumption is that you are intending to use everyone in the group who wishes to take part. You need to be sure that you have the people who can take on the most demanding roles, but also need to have enough interesting work for the less experienced. If the play has plenty of opportunities for ensemble work, the less assured members will not feel underused and be able to develop their abilities in new areas.

A serious play makes demands on its actors which will have to be matched by a degree of emotional maturity. Most youth theatre groups which have been established for some time will be capable of meeting these demands. Some school groups likewise, but on the whole it is better to give younger groups material which comes within their emotional range. However, a youth theatre group with a wide age range, say fourteen to nineteen, and a well established membership, can cope with a text which may seem beyond the immediate comprehension of the younger members, as the group awareness is likely to be dominated by the older members, and the younger ones, working with them, undergo a growth in emotional maturity and understanding which they could not achieve if they were restricted to contact with their immediate peer group. This opens a wider range of possibilities in the choice of play.

As you are likely to have more knowledge of the repertoire than the young people you are working with, it is more likely that you will be the one to suggest a certain text, or choice of texts. An older group may well have some suggestions, or at least have some knowledge of the plays you are considering, or of their writers. It is worth opening discussions on a possible text at a very early stage, well before you are planning to begin rehearsals. This will allow a reasonable amount of discussion. They can read the play if they wish to, and at any rate you can 'tell the story' and give them a general idea of the nature of the play, its themes, and possible approaches to it. If their enthusiasm is fired at this stage, fine. If you get a negative or pallid response, it is better to drop that idea and look for a new one. However keen you may be to work on a particular text, if they don't like it you are in for months of drudgery and, most likely, a disappearing cast.

The same holds good for a play that just one or two of the group are suggesting, or enthuse over. Unless the choice of play is made together, it is not worth making.

This may sound like a daunting task, with too many hurdles to negotiate. In fact, it can be an exciting and positive process, the start of a new venture, in which you will all have the opportunity to explore ideas and use language which someone else has set down, but which you can interpret and present in your own way.

Introducing the play to the group

A certain formality about the introduction of the script can mark the opening of the production period. Although you will have discussed it with them during the selection process, and some may have read it already, this enables everyone to participate in the first encounter between play and players on an equal footing, and to share the initial reactions.

You will, of course, need to have sufficient copies of the text for everyone, or at least one between two, and if the play is a long one you may also need to have made the preliminary rough cuts, so that they can understand how the play will work.

An introductory technique which works well and has the benefit of complete egalitarianism is to read the play round a circle. Everyone takes a speech in turn. The longer ones can be split on an ad hoc basis. Don't give the cuts before you start (except perhaps for very large sections). Just announce each as you come to it.

This has advantages over allocating parts for the whole read-through, or even a section at a time. Even though you may actively avoid indicating possible casting, assumptions will be made if you make choices for this particular exercise, and at this stage you really need to be playing on an open field, even though you are likely to have some ideas about whom you want to play what. Both dominant and quieter individuals are being treated with complete equality, and how much they have to read, and which parts, will be a matter of chance. The overall concentration level is likely to be higher than if individuals can switch off for a whole scene.

It also provides you with some initial information. Who can lift the text from the page and make it his or her own? Which voices show an affinity with which words? Which voices seem to balance, or contrast with, others? Which speeches, and which sections of the play, reveal difficulties in interpretation? Which parts of the play do they particularly enjoy at this first reading? Which ones make them switch off?

It may be that the play is too long to read as a whole in one session. It may also happen that they show a desire to begin working on certain sections, and you need to be alert to the mood and the needs of the group to make the best use of their enthusiasm. If you don't manage to read through the whole play together, that's fine, and they can finish it by themselves, but you should aim to deal with a substantial amount.

It is useful, however, to spend a little time discussing their reactions to what they have read, what they feel about the language of the play, the characters, the themes and the plot. If you have cut the text, it may be that some of the cuts will have to be reviewed in the light of this discussion. Some areas may need cuts restored for clarity, other cuts may be made of material which is not essential and does not appeal. This early discussion will begin to establish ideas about the style of production, altering or reinforcing ideas which emerged during the choice of play. You are also likely to get some indication of which characters particular individuals are interested in and would like to work on, which may help in casting decisions.

Workshops

Now that the play, its themes, plot and characters are established in everyone's mind, it is possible to take some time working alongside the text, rather than allowing the text to dominate activities. As with devised work, much of the success of the production will depend on the skills in improvisation and characterisation which have formed the basis of past work, but which can now be drawn on selectively as they are relevant to the production. It is possible that some text-based work will be appropriate at this stage, but it can well be delayed for a while. If it is incorporated, it should be chosen for its relevance to the workshop practice, just as that is used for its relevance to the different aspects of the play.

Working on the assumption that everyone has a reasonable knowledge of the text, and has read a sizeable amount of it, you can isolate certain themes and characters to place at the centre of this phase of the work. Many of the games and exercises described in Chapters 2 and 3 can be adapted, but these are a few suggestions which may be useful.

● In pairs, devise a ten-word script based on a theme from the play, and give the script to another pair to play.

● Use key theme words to trigger instant improvisation, single, in pairs, and in small groups.

● Work on a developed improvisation using a situation or theme from the play.

- Sit in a circle, and go through the alphabet, a word for each person, using words associated in any way with the play. Challenges can be made for unlikely words, which may lead to some interesting discussion.

- In small groups, produce a tableau which expresses some aspect of the play. If one member of the group acts as 'sculptor' he can then give an explanation or guided tour of the work.

- Each person, individually and secretly, chooses to be one character from the play. Play status games, such as walking with and without eye contact, finding the right place in a status line, walking towards another person in a narrow space. Run through a series of these games quickly, then ask everyone to reveal their character and discuss what happened. Alternatively, write the names of characters on slips of paper and stick them onto people's foreheads, not allowing them to see who they are. Then play the same games and observe and discuss reactions. They may well guess who they are before the games are over. If not, finding out can be part of the discussion.

- Each person takes on a role and, working in twos and threes, places the characters in different situations, such as a lift, a 'bus queue, park bench, customs post.

- In a circle, re-tell the story of the play, each person contributing in turn.

- Choose several aspects of the play, such as characters, key episodes or themes, as the subjects for an expand/contract version of *Just a Minute*.

These activities may reveal some new aspects of the play and possibilities for the production. They may also throw up queries about interpretation. The opportunities for early exploration and discoveries are very useful, but this stage of the process should not be rested at for too long. Two or three sessions are quite adequate if the activities are not taking place alongside some work on the script. They do not, however, need to be cut off completely, and sometimes, if you have come across a block in working on a particular section of the play, this can be removed by switching to a different, though parallel, activity for a short time.

At this stage, in-depth character work is not appropriate, because until an actor has done some work on a role he has little to bring to the more extensive exercises, but the suggestions above will help the group to familiarise themselves with the characters, and gain an awareness of their relative status and relationships with each other.

Exploring the text

If you take this approach (or one based on these ideas) as the basis of your production process, you will still not have cast the play, and there is still no need to do so, as the longer the group spends working together, in small groups and individually, on all aspects of the play the better they will know it and the easier they will find the later stages of intensive work.

You will probably have gleaned many ideas about the probable style and detail of the production from watching them work and from discussions, as well as your own thoughts about the play. It is worth keeping some record of these, both for yourself and on some more public notice board if they are crucial for future reference. Photographing some of the tableaux, for instance, is very useful.

This stage, when you begin to focus more closely on the text, will give you even more ideas, and recording them will become more important. However, they should still be just that – ideas. Don't fix anything too early. Even though you may all feel that a certain interpretation which emerges early on cannot be improved, as the work develops it may not fit into the overall concept, and have to be reconsidered.

As with a devised play, it is important to keep the impression of freshness; that this is the first time this scene has been played, or these words spoken. If you can allow the right degree of freedom in playing up to and including performance, you may well achieve this.

The exploration of the text need not be exhaustive, but it should range quite widely throughout the play, focusing on key scenes which vary in nature. Scenes in which relationships are central, others in which narrative or action predominate. You may wish to take a fairly long scene and split it into smaller sections, giving each section to a small group to work on, and then play them consecutively. Shorter scenes can be given to groups in their entirety, to provide alternative interpretations for discussion.

But straight playing of the different scenes is not the only approach. Here are some further suggestions.

- Select a key incident, create a tableau to express it. Act the scene, either using the text or improvising, up to the tableau, freeze the action at that point. Alternatively, use the tableau at the beginning of the action.

- Select three crucial moments from a short scene. Play the scene, freezing the action momentarily at those points.

- Using a passage of dialogue for two characters, have a second pair play the sub-text, either in mime, or spoken between the lines of the text.

- Find one essential property, item of costume or stage furniture relevant to a particular scene, and play the scene using that as the main focus.

- Play the scene in mime, with one person acting as commentator on the action.

- If the script has passages of chorus work, explore different ways of using this, using movement, and varying combinations of voices.

The object of this work is not to find 'clever' ways of using the text, nor to be startling or innovative for its own sake, but to attempt to establish the partnership between play and players which was mentioned earlier. Given the freedom to experiment – and according to the nature and experience of the group experimentation can go much further than suggested – a deeper understanding of the text will emerge without the need for lengthy, theoretical debate. As the essence of theatre is performance, this is where the emphasis should be put throughout the rehearsal process. Discussion is also necessary, but any purely cerebral activity should play a secondary role in the process of re-creating an existing play.

During this stage, as well as exploring the text and gathering ideas about playing, you will be observing how individuals work together, how well they handle the demands of particular roles, which combinations and groups work together best. This knowledge will be invaluable to you when you come to cast the play.

This is also the stage at which you will need to decide about other aspects of the production, such as the use of music, and begin consultations about this with the relevant people.

Casting

If you are working with a well-established group, it is likely that
you will be choosing the most experienced to play the major roles.
Youth theatres usually work on something like an apprenticeship
system. New members learn much from the longer-serving
members, and don't expect to take large parts in a production.
However, it often happens that you have relatively new people
who have some natural, raw talent which can be used in major
roles, and if so they should be given this opportunity. Young
people are very perceptive, and they are likely to recognise why
you may have given a newcomer a certain part to play, especially if
there has been quite a long run-in period before you cast the play.
Some parts may demand particular skills, such as a good,
confident, singing voice, which will also affect your decision.

Outside pressures, such as public examinations, may also affect
your choice, and you may find that some of your longest-serving
and most reliable people will be happy to take cameo roles, which
put less pressure on them, and which they can enjoy without
having to make too many choices about how to use their available
free time, thus avoiding school and parental conflict!

By now, you will have seen most of your potential cast in action
dealing with different characters and sections of the play, so any
auditioning process will have taken place without any formality.
You may still, however, be put in the position of disappointing
some people, who may have shown either openly or surreptitiously
that they want to play certain parts for which they are not suited, or
which you feel that others can handle better. This is never easy to
deal with. It is not pleasant to disappoint someone who is loyal and
hard-working, but if your relationship with them is good, the
disappointment can be dealt with on an individual basis by giving
an honest explanation.

When casting, it's worthwhile doing it all at once. This means
that, if you are dealing with a play in which most if not all the cast
play more than one role, such as minor parts in crowd scenes, they
are told precisely what those are when the cast list is published.
Though there is likely to be some swapping around at a later stage,
it means that everything is covered initially, and they know exactly
what they are doing and which scenes they are involved in
throughout the play. This makes for smooth running of rehearsals
later on.

Publish the cast list and give everyone a written copy so that the information can be assimilated and, if necessary, explained. At the same time as you do this, you can make everyone's life easier if you produce a second sheet of information on which the play is broken down into sections, which may run across scene divisions if you have cut the play. Give the names of the characters involved in each section, together with any necessary detail. Your rehearsal schedule can then be based on this, and you can see at a glance which people you need at any time. This avoids the problem of people standing around with nothing to do while you work with others.

The information sheet will probably look something like this:-

The Caucasian Chalk Circle

section 1a (pages 9 – 12)	city streets	Singer/Governor/Governor's wife/Fat Prince/Adjutant/doctors/soldiers/crowd/rider
section 1b (pages 12 – 13)	palace gateway	Singer/Grusha/Simon
section 1c (pages 14 – 16)	outside palace	Singer/Governor/Governor's wife/Fat Prince/Adjutant/architects/rider/soldiers

and so on.

Choice of staging

As with a devised play, you will want to choose how to set the play at quite an early stage, so that rehearsals can be undertaken realistically. You may not be rehearsing in the space you will be performing in, and this does have some advantages, as although it is good to get used to the playing venue, its acoustics and its general atmosphere, a restrictive space, such as the stage of a school hall, can cramp your style by imposing a certain shape and style on the production.

Even if you are expected to play in the school hall, look at it with fresh eyes. Do you have to use the stage? If you do, can you build out from it to make a more interesting shape? What kind of relationship do you want with the audience? Do you want them watching from a distance, or do you want them close to the action? How about a promenade production? If you are going for this style, how do you handle the audience, and how do you move them around to create space for the action?

If you are going for promenade, in the round, transverse, or any similar kind of 'shape' you will need to think about just what you will need within the playing area. To play everything flat on the floor can be boring, realistic sets are out, but if you have too many raised areas there is the danger of blocking many of the audience's sightlines. Small stage blocks and light rostra which can be moved during the course of performance are one solution. Alternatively, one permanent raised area, with the audience placed so that it can see all the action, can solve some of these problems.

When deciding on the shape of the playing area, bear in mind also the places at which the players will get on and off. They may need to move behind the audience to get to a new entrance. Is there adequate room? If there are to be costume changes, where will these take place? A screen may be adequate: find the right place for it in the overall design of the performance area. Properties and their positions relative to use must also be considered.

One of the simplest solutions to a lot of staging problems is to have everyone and everything 'on stage' for the whole of the action, with costume changes, collection of props and so on taking place in full view of the audience. Whether this is feasible will depend very much on the style of production, and whatever your choice the shape, size and nature of your staging must be integral to the overall concept, and it is worth spending time thinking about and discussing this. If it does involve close contact with the audience, the cast needs to be reminded of this throughout rehearsals, so that they can find ways of using the opportunities that this gives. And once rehearsals begin they should take place within a mock-up of the intended playing area, which can be taped out on the floor and the blocks and rostra (or substitute) used from the start.

Any style other than flat-on playing does give the director problems, as instead of remaining in once place during rehearsals it is necessary to move around constantly to see how things look from other angles. You can use extra pairs of eyes for this, with everyone who is not working in a particular scene deputed to watch it from another point. The advantage is that the playing can be far freer, with the whole of the space, or sections of it, used in a natural way, and some exciting patterns of movement can be developed.

Early rehearsals, organisation and method

When the basic decisions have been made about the nature and style of production, the groundwork done on the text, and the play cast, you will be beginning a more formal rehearsal process. The length of this intensive rehearsal period will depend on the play itself and the number of hours you can realistically give to it. Days and times for rehearsals must be discussed with the group. It is no use scheduling whole-day rehearsals for Saturdays if some of the cast have jobs then. A very rough guide is that with a moderately experienced group you should be able to prepare a two-hour play over a period of three to four months, starting with one two-hour session a week, and gradually increasing the length and frequency of sessions as the production dates come closer.

Your early rehearsal period should be designed to deal with the whole of the text. The later period is when you take things to pieces again, re-examine and re-work them intensively. But if you can work towards a complete run-through, however rough, two-thirds of the way through the period, you should be on course to complete the work satisfactorily.

When you have worked out a realistic early rehearsal schedule, taking into account any intervening holiday periods and unavoidable absences which members of the cast tell you about in advance, have it printed and give everyone a copy, which they need to show to their parents so that their commitment is understood.

The schedule should give the dates and times of rehearsals, the sections to be dealt with, who is needed at what times, and cover any specialist rehearsals, such as for music. Show the point from which no books will be used, so that they have plenty of advance warning.

It is important to plan the rehearsals to make use of everyone there: that is, do not call people for two o'clock when you know that you will not be reaching that part of the play in which they are involved until four o'clock. If your workshop venue has other rooms where people can go when they are not needed, this is perhaps not so important, and the social aspects of the work cannot be forgotten. Most groups are composed of people who enjoy each other's company, and are quite happy to spend time gossiping (or even learning their lines!). But if there is only one space, it is distracting and bad practice to have people sitting in corners talking when you are trying to work seriously with others.

Although you will be giving full details later of the arrangements for final rehearsals and performance dates and times, make sure that these are known to the group as soon as they have been fixed.

Rehearsal methods will develop naturally and be determined by the results of the earlier workshopping of the script. There will be parts which you will not have touched on, but how these are tackled will probably develop naturally from your initial ideas. You will, to an extent, be linking together the concepts and approaches which have already been established, and thus new work will be done in the same style.

They should be encouraged to work without a script in hand as soon as realistically possible. Holding a book, or papers, inhibits movement, and some people will use a script to hide behind, if they are uncertain about getting to grips with the real acting. You need to be fairly ruthless about the 'no books after' rule. It is better to prompt for these rehearsals than allow scripts to be used up to the last minute. Again, more experienced people will take the lead in abandoning the script, as they feel inhibited by it, and this will set the precedent for others.

Remember to teach newcomers how to learn a script. Give them tips on strategies, such as using a taperecorder if they find it helps, and, most importantly that they learn their cues as well as their speeches, and are familiar with what everyone says throughout each scene they are involved in.

It is advisable not to be too zealous about total fidelity to the printed words. Of course, in some cases, such as Shakespeare's plays, it is essential that the original words are used exactly, but in many other cases, especially with prose works, you are likely to find that slight changes and substitutions occur which make no difference to the sense of the original, and which the speaker obviously feels comfortable with. As the most important thing is that they should tell the story of the play, it is better to allow them to tell their own version in places than to insist on a pedantic, word-for-word, rendition of the original text.

By concentrating on one section at a time, you may find that in one rehearsal you will be dealing with parts of the script which are familiar and others which are new. One method of approach is to run the familiar material in the way which has been chosen, and then to work straight on into the new, giving the actors the responsibility of playing it as they feel that it flows. Their instinctive use of the script and the acting opportunities it provides will often be the right one, and then the director's task is to make the slight adjustments that seem necessary to make the scene work. They need to be comfortable with what they are doing, and this is most likely to come about if they are given the freedom to experiment and offer approaches than if you come to rehearsal armed with a set of moves, actions and reactions, and seek to impose them.

The practice of blocking a scene is one which can impede this natural development. Obviously, the movement of actors within the playing area is subject to certain disciplines. Pre-arranged groupings are essential at times, actors have to get into and out of a scene efficiently and naturally, but if they are all involved in playing the scene and telling the story most of these essential moves will arise spontaneously, and are likely to be correct. Adjustments of timing and angles of playing can be put in place quickly and simply as the scene is rehearsed.

Initially, all they need to know is where to come from, when, and where everyone else is likely to be. Awareness of the position and needs of the audience must also be built in at this stage, and if this is kept in mind you can allow them to make their own moves driven by the impetus and energies of the scene they are playing.

At times, you may find it useful to read through a new scene together before starting to work on it, but everyone should by now be working on the assumption that the material is familiar to all the cast. A brief discussion about what is happening in the scene, the general mood, and the function of the protagonists can precede the first working, but doing it, rather than talking about it, should be the rule during rehearsals.

During this period, you may want to do some more intensive work on characterisation. If you are working with a large group, this can be a problem, as there may be a number whose function within the play does not depend on a developed characterisation. It is probably wisest to hold a separate session with just those people who need such work, so that they can work on exploring the characters they are playing, using techniques such as status games and hot-seating exercises.

There are a number of other strategies which you may find useful during this rehearsal period. What you choose will depend on the play and the style of playing, and any problems you encounter during the work. You may want to repeat some of the strategies used in the workshopping period for those parts which are being dealt with for the first time, but they must be specifically chosen to be appropriate to your requirements.

These are some other possibilities for particular needs.

A scene involving emotional conflict between two characters

● Play the scene with both keeping close physical contact with each other, then as far apart from each other as space allows.

● Play 'touch back tag' while speaking the words, in character.

● Sit back to back, speak the words slowly, loudly, without expression.

● Put the script aside and improvise the scene, perhaps using numbers instead of words.

The detached, somewhat surrealistic approach can give the actors new insights and, especially in the case of young actors, help to overcome any embarrassment. They can then tackle the scene again and play it straight with increased experience and awareness.

A scene in which two or more defined groups of characters are involved, each taking up the dialogue in turn

● Each group plays through the whole of its dialogue simultaneously, with no pauses. This results in a great deal of confused noise but each group maintains its energies.

● Using a ball or beanbag, group A passes it from hand to hand as they speak, then throws it to the first speaker in group B, and so on.

(● Swap scripts. Group A plays B's words, B plays C's, and so on.

● Play the scene with everyone in a tight, physically touching group, then as far apart as possible, even using screens between the groups if you have them.

This enables everyone to be fully aware of the words and actions of others in the scene, and facilitates the interaction between groups.

Ensemble work

●   Everyone walks at random around the room, saying their lines in turn.

●   Colour-code by giving tickets of the same colour to people who make up each sub-group within the whole, so that they can recognise each other and move together to exchange their parts of the dialogue.

●   Give each sub-group a territory in the area, from which they move and to which they return.

●   Shout the dialogue, then whisper it.

This helps to find a natural pattern of movement and words within a scene, and makes everyone aware of whom they relate to most frequently.

These are just a few suggestions and by no means a comprehensive list. The aim is to allow them to find ways of solving problems, for them to discover the natural rhythms within the different situations which the script imposes. Their confidence in their own work is enhanced by giving them this responsibility, and they can thus continue to develop their ideas throughout the rehearsal period.

To summarise, the working session on a particular section could be organised as follows.

(a)   Briefly read over and/or discuss the section, or a part of it.

(b)   Play it, without interruption, perhaps topping and tailing it with work previously prepared.

(c)   Pause to discuss any difficulties you or they have identified.

(d)   If appropriate, use one or more of the strategies suggested there.

(e)   Play the scene again, this time stopping to make adjustments.

(f)   Final run-through of the scene, with everything that has been worked on taken into account.

A steady working through the play, not necessarily in order from start to finish but using the sections you have split the play into, in ways which both give some coherence and vary the nature of the work, should give the confidence for a complete run-through at the two-thirds stage of the rehearsal period.

Individual and ensemble work

The previous paragraphs have mentioned some aspects of individual and ensemble work which need to be considered during the rehearsal period. However, there are some further aspects which should be taken into account.

As far as individual work is concerned, those of us who take on the responsibility of theatre work with young people soon recognise that we are sometimes putting them into situations of emotional stress. Not just the stress of performing, but the stress of taking on a role of a character whose emotional life makes certain demands on a young actor. Obviously, the choice of actor for role will have taken this into account. We do not overburden those who are not prepared or are unable to cope with these demands. Nevertheless, even with the comparatively experienced and mature young actor, it is necessary to be alert to any stress which he or she may be undergoing as a result of taking on such a role, and the particular difficulties associated with it.

Such an actor needs some of your time, understanding and expertise. If there are areas of characterisation which he needs to explore in order to play the part effectively, he will be helped by the exercises mentioned earlier, carried out under your guidance and with a small supportive group, who can discover things together about the relationships, background and motivations of the people they are playing. Give them time for such intensive work and discussion away from the rest of the group, and this time may need to be fairly long, though probably not open-ended. You may find that some discussion on a one-to-one basis is also sought, and should be prepared to give time for this.

If the play has some episodes whose content is sensitive and emotionally charged, it is always best to provide some privacy for the early work on these. It is inhibiting, even for very experienced actors, to take the first steps onto dangerous ground before a group of uninvolved spectators. You should make it possible for the early work on such scenes to be done by the actors concerned either totally on their own (if that is their wish) or with only you present. This should not be prolonged to the stage of self-indulgence, but allows them to become confident and familiar with that they are doing before it is seen by others.

It can happen with some young actors that they become over-immersed in their roles. This is seldom harmful in the long run, but may have some short-term effects which we need to be aware of, and have ways of dealing with.

This usually occurs when the actor and the character he is playing have some psychological similarities. And as casting is often dependent on what is seen as an actor's suitability for a role, this is always a possibility. It can produce a situation of conflict, when fictional antagonisms from the play become extended into real-life relationships of those playing certain parts. Conversely, it can intensify special relationships which may have existed before, but which are given an emotional impetus by the fictional relationship.

Undoubtedly, the heightened emotional intensity which can be brought to a role can make for very exciting theatre, but a balance must be achieved. The actor must be helped to re-discover and use this awareness and these energies for performance, at the same time being able to set them aside while living his normal life.

These situations require careful handling. Even if you do not suspect that they are incipient, it is worth ensuring that any intensive character work is 'talked down' at the end of a session, and that the work ends with an energy-releasing and non-cerebral game. A sense of humour, on your part and that of the cast in general, is a great asset, providing that it is not invoked in a way which damages any individual or devalues the work you are engaged on. As in all aspects of this work, much depends on healthy and trusting relationships within the group, and yours with them individually and as a whole.

Unsurprisingly, potential problems with ensemble work may be diametrically opposed in nature to those you may have with individuals. To achieve effective and exciting use of large groups demands some skills in choreography from the director. There will be the need to blend and balance naturalistic and stylised groupings and movement, while giving the impression of spontaneity and ease.

Perhaps it is at this stage that the director's role seems at its most dictatorial, and the trick is to bring about a fusion between the suggestions which come from the group, either in discussion or in physical work, and what you feel will make effective theatre.

In doing this, it can happen that individuals, usually newcomers and the less experienced, may feel undervalued because you are placing less emphasis on the people who make up the group than the whole. This can lead to loss of interest and therefore concentration, diminishing the overall quality that can be achieved.

Again, good communication can help to overcome such difficulties. If you choose relevant games and exercises to try out ideas about movement and groupings, and discuss the effects you are aiming for, you are likely to hold their interest more than if you go in with a pre-determined plan which they feel is being imposed on them.

It is important that they are aware of the function and focus of group work. Are they offering commentary, or moving the action forward? Are they a group of separate characters, or more anonymous and cohesive, like a chorus? Are they involved or uninvolved emotionally with the action? How do they relate to each other, to the other characters on stage, to the audience?

The nature of ensemble work and the kind of use you will make of it is dependent on the nature of the production. It can provide exciting challenges for everyone involved, to find new ways of handling material. The technique of sharing it out with a line for everyone has become something of a cliché, though it can be effective in small doses, and be dramatically relevant. If any choral work is involved, you can experiment with different blendings of voices, different rhythms and timings. It is important not to underestimate the amount of rehearsal time that is needed to make ensemble work really effective, because new skills have to be learned and practised. Vocal work and movement have to be matched. Tableaux, freezes, repetitive movement, and the use of varying speeds are all possibilities.

Above all, the importance of everyone who is on stage needs to be reinforced. They need to be reminded constantly that each one of them is visible to the audience, and needs to be totally involved in the action at all times.

First run-through

As the date of the first run-through approaches, it is a good idea to check over the administrative and technical side of the production. You will most likely have delegated responsibilities for the various aspects to members of the group and/or other helpers, but unless you have the luxury of a producer in overall charge you are the person at the centre of the network who will have initiated the various processes, and you are ultimately responsible if anything goes wrong.

A production check list is given in the last section of this book. You can use this to focus on the various areas, but even if you have already set in motion most of this work, you should call a production meeting to reassure yourself that everything is in hand.

If you are performing in your own venue, there will be some things which you will not need to check, but it is still worthwhile ensuring in advance that everyone can get in, and home, on the days of the final rehearsals and performance nights. This is also one of the rare occasions on which you may wish to enlist parental help, as drivers, front of house staff, for poster distribution. Your final rehearsal/production schedule can include a request for help to parents, as well as ensuring that they are aware of the commitment their children have made for the production period.

For the first run-through of the play, try to use as much as you have available of properties and set, though costume is not so important. This is the first opportunity you will have to assess how well the production holds together, how it flows, the overall rhythm, the strengths and weaknesses, and the playing time. You will have the opportunity to identify any problems with staging, exits and entrances, which can be overcome before the final rehearsals.

Except in extreme emergencies, no scripts should be used. There are bound to be plenty of prompts, but this is unimportant as long as the narrative moves forward and the cast can begin to feel the pace of the play. This first run-through usually has the effect of enhancing everyone's awareness of what they are undertaking. For some people, it may be the first time they have seen parts of the play, and can experience it as a dramatic entity. They will see the part that their own work plays in the overall concept. They can appreciate more fully the work of others, and recognise how the early ideas and experiments have been brought together to make a coherent whole.

It is also likely to have a fairly sobering effect. Their initial assessment of how things are going will probably be on the lines of 'that was terrible', or a more succinct expression. But after the immediate reaction you can encourage a more constructive and reasoned analysis. Those who have gone through the process before tend to be more realistic, knowing that what they have created at this time is akin to the first draft of a poem, the initial sketches for a painting. Encourage them to share this knowledge with the less experienced, and give them your own considered assessment of the stage you have reached together, how far you have to go, and how you are going to attain your goals.

Having identified the major areas which need more intensive work, draw up a schedule for the final rehearsals, giving details also of performance venues and call times, and distribute this as soon as possible.

Last rehearsals

However little time you feel you have left for the amount of work you feel is necessary, it is important not to let the atmosphere of the final rehearsals get heavy. There should still be some opportunity for experimentation, especially in areas which you are unhappy about at the run-through. This will take far less time than in the earlier stages, because everyone will know the play well now, and recognise what is needed and what works.

If you do feel that the time allows and that it would be useful, take them back to their initial ideas, and let them see how these have developed, and whether anything has been lost that needs to be replaced. Otherwise, the adjustments you will be making are of detail rather than whole scenes.

Though you want to spend time working intensively on certain sections, make opportunities to re-run extended sections of the play. The increased familiarity will give confidence to the cast, and you will find that individual performances will gain in strength and conviction, even though you have not concentrated on them individually.

Keep a running check on characterisation. Has it developed consistently? Are all the actions and speeches true to the personae that have been created?

Is the ensemble work developing at the same rate as the individual? Sharpen up cues and patterns of movement.

Ensure that the pace, shape and tensions within scenes and through longer sections are recognised and understood by everyone.

As the final rehearsals progress, make opportunities to work as intensively on any other aspects of performance, such as music and dance, as you are on the acting, so that the performance standard is uniform.

Try to organise the schedule to allow two more complete run-throughs of the play before the dress rehearsal. The more often they can experience working the play as a whole the more confident they will become, so that they can relax and enjoy the public performances, knowing that they can work supportively and give their best as individuals.

Are you going to need a prompt? It is far better if you can manage without one, but for a long play with a demanding script it may be best to give them the security of knowing that it will be there in an emergency. If you are going to have one, choose someone intelligent and sympathetic, and ensure that he sits in on several of the last rehearsals, so that he knows how the play works and the pace of the speeches. Nothing is more off-putting that an unnecessary prompt in a dramatic pause.

If the cast know that their overriding tasks are to tell the story to the audience, to drive the action forward, and to play the scene, you will find that they become adept at covering any mistakes that occur, and support each other so effectively that, though you may know when something has gone wrong, no one else will. I once had a cast which improvised the whole of the last ten minutes of a play when an essential property went missing on stage, and no one in the audience suspected that anything was amiss.

During this final phase of preparation, you will need to help them maintain an impetus which moves the work towards its culmination in public performance. A lot of encouragement is needed, praise balanced by constructive analysis and criticism. If they still enjoy the work, after so much concentrated effort, that is an achievement in itself, and that enjoyment will convey itself to their audience.

Chapter 7

Approaches to performance

The final approaches to performance are the same whether you are working on a devised or a scripted play. This step by step account may well cover matters which are familiar to anyone who has experience of working on a production with young people. But if you have not done it before, or have worked either with professional actors or adult amateur groups, it is possible that there are some matters which have not occurred to you, which are relevant when working with a young company, but may not be so important in other circumstances.

These approaches have been tried and tested with many youth groups, and do seem to aid the smooth running and enjoyment of a production. Of course, everyone's circumstances are different. You may, for example, rehearse in one venue and play in another, so that you cannot have all your technical facilities to hand until the dress rehearsal. You may tour your work, which means setting up in different venues every night, and arranging group transport. Different conditions bring different needs and pressures, but planning and clear dissemination of information on a need-to-know basis will make your work easier.

Your final rehearsals should be undertaken in as professional a manner as possible. If everything has gone according to plan – or something approaching that! – the group probably will have undergone a subtle change in its collective personality. The disciplines which have been built into the process will have gone a long way towards changing it from a group of young people into something like a theatre company, with individuals taking on responsibility for their own work, and for the success of the group as a whole. In the final run down to performance, they should be treated as a company, and will respond to this approach.

It is important that they understand the demands and nature of these final stages, especially newcomers who will be doing it for the first time. If the details were not given on the rehearsal schedule, you need to give them a final written notice with times for the technical rehearsal, the dress rehearsal, and the call times for performances. Make sure that any problems with transport have been dealt with, to avoid any last minute panic.

During your last rehearsals, use essential costume, especially if changes have to be made, so that these can be practised. Properties too: know when and where they are needed, so that their positions backstage or on set are established and familiar to everyone.

Check costume and properties generally, decide on any make-up needed, and ensure that one person is in charge of the make-up box.

Technical rehearsal

Who you will need to attend the technical rehearsal will depend on the nature of the show. Lighting and stage crew, of course. The lighting plot will already have been fixed, also sound cues if you are using any recorded material. If you are using live music, and lighting cues are linked to this in any way, you may need at least one of the musicians present so that smooth cuing can be achieved. Otherwise, you only need a few bodies around to take stage positions, to enable the focusing and balancing of lights.

Once the lighting set is up, lamps focused, and the stage set is in position, run through the whole show on a technical basis from cue to cue. Pay particular attention to the opening and closing sequences, establish signals, and make sure that someone is covering house lights if these are not controlled from the lighting desk. Check the sound levels, both of recorded and live music.

Spend some time with the stage manager. Establish the positions of properties, and where any backstage staff will be during performance. If you are using a prompt, set up his position, and ensure that he has light. Some torches for backstage are a must.

It is important to allow plenty of time for the technical rehearsal. If you try to get through it from start to finish in a couple of hours before the dress rehearsal you will almost inevitably find that something goes wrong, your cast will arrive before you have finished, and you will have a disgruntled set of technicians who feel undervalued. Their importance to the success of the production cannot be overestimated, so it is worthwhile cosseting them a bit beforehand.

Dress rehearsal

The dress rehearsal should be regarded as a performance, using all costume, make-up, properties, lighting and effects. Call the cast for a time which bears the same relationship to the start time that will obtain for public performances. If you have an interval, again, allow the right amount of time for this.

To new members, the discipline of the dress rehearsal may come as a surprise, but it will prepare them well for the public performance. For the experienced, it will be a reminder.

This is the stage at which many directors remember that they have not yet organised the curtain call, and it is the last chance to do so. Make it as simple as possible, in keeping with the mood of the performance, and never allow it to last too long. Run through the routine before the start of the rehearsal.

You may want to invite a small number of people to provide an audience. It is best to be selective about this. A large crowd of friends and families, who are not dispersed amongst a larger audience, does not provide a good atmosphere, and can be very inhibiting.

This may be the first time that make-up is used. Apart from anything special, which should have been practised beforehand, it should be as simple as possible, but some people may need assistance if they have never applied it before. More experienced members can be asked to oversee and help where necessary. Check the make-up under lights before you start to run the show.

Prepare the cast to go on with a short concentration exercise, and then run the play as for the public. Try to dispel the old myth about the bad dress rehearsal ensuring a good first night. It is not a useful maxim. It is true that this is really the last opportunity to make any avoidable mistakes in comparative privacy, but on the whole confidence will be greater if mistakes are not made. On the other hand, if things do go wrong you will need to boost their confidence, without making them feel that mistakes don't matter. A good dress performance can be very reassuring, but that too needs a well judged reaction, to avoid any possible smugness in the company. Your reaction to what they do must be carefully attuned to what you perceive as their emotional needs.

Don't give notes in the interval, unless they are essential for the running of the second half. A brief mention about diction and voice levels may be appropriate, but otherwise save the notes until the end, when they have got over their initial reactions, ecstatic or despairing.

Keep your notes as brief and encouraging as possible, whatever you may feel. Come what may, they are the ones who are going to have to play before an audience, not you. They will know as well as you do what went wrong, and why. It is best to be general rather than specific to individual performances. If anything does need to be said to individuals, try to do so privately.

Wish them well, remind them of call times, and tell them to get a good night's sleep.

Performance

Technicians and backstage staff should be called half an hour before the actors, so that they can make a final check on lights and sound, and ensure that the areas which are used as dressing rooms are ready for use.

It is perhaps worth mentioning here how to cope with the ultimate emergency. A member of the cast, perhaps someone with a major role, is unavailable at the last minute – for whatever reason. This could be as late as half an hour before the performance. It is very unusual for youth groups to use understudies, so what do you do?

Much will depend on the nature of the play, but if you have a large cast your best course is to choose someone reliable who has a minor role, is not immediately involved with the missing character, and get him to play the part from the book. This may necessitate others cutting or doubling up on other parts, but if you have a group which has worked well together and is confident in their knowledge of the play, they can cope with this with surprising ease.

If this is completely impossible, and there is nobody on whom you can call who knows not just the play but also the production, should you step in yourself? It is perhaps best to leave this decision to the group. It is their play now, and they should be given the chance to discuss the problem and you should be guided by their feelings.

The most important thing to remember in these circumstances is that the emergency must be dealt with calmly, and you will need to cope firmly, though sympathetically, with any incipient panic. If they feel that it is a situation which they can handle in a sensible and professional manner, that will do a great deal for their morale.

It is also worthwhile making it a rule that nobody talks about feeling nervous. Tell them in advance that it is a natural feeling, that they are likely to perform better with a bit of adrenalin running through their veins, but that it is self-indulgent and counterproductive to talk about one's own feelings and thereby stimulate an atmosphere of tension, in which tempers can easily be lost.

The actors should have been called a full hour before the scheduled starting time for the performance. Let them go into the acting area and hold a voice check before they dress and make up. If you can make the atmosphere for this relaxed and enjoyable, yet workmanlike, it helps establish the right mood. You will have discovered already if there are any problems with the acoustics in the space, and be able to alert them to these. One technique you can use is to get each of them to 'take a line across the stage'. Do this quite fast, only stopping proceedings if someone's voice level needs adjusting.

If the show includes singing, run through a group number that they all enjoy, and encourage any soloists to try out their voices in the space.

As director, you should really fade into the background now and leave it all to the stage manager, but in practice, with a young company, it is better to stay around and keep an eye on things, ready to calm down any friction which may arise from nervous tension. Give an unobtrusive countdown, especially letting them know when the house is open and they cannot go forward any longer. This is particularly important if the only available toilets are front of house.

About ten minutes before the start bring everyone together, and talk them through a gentle warm-up and concentration exercise, helping them to focus their energies on the performance, making them feel that you have every confidence in them.

During the performance, it is worthwhile taking some notes as it runs, but only of very specific points that you know can be adjusted. Don't give these at the interval or after the show – unless it is imperative. Save them for the talk-in to the next performance. Probably the only notes that are justified at the interval are on voice levels, if necessary.

However well or badly the performance goes, you will need to tailor your reaction to the needs of the company. If anything went wrong, talk through it carefully, resisting any attempt to apportion blame. If they performed extremely well, give praise, but don't allow them to become complaisant. Your reactions to the first performance can set the standard for subsequent ones.

Finally, don't allow them to forget the disciplines of practicalities in their euphoria or despair. Dressing rooms must be cleared, or left tidy, make-up and costumes ready for the next performance. And they will need reminding of the next day's call time before you go on to talk to the technicians about how it was for them.

Resources and information

A short compendium of items referred to earlier in the text, advice on the legal and other aspects of theatre work, and some useful addresses.

Workshop and Course Models

1. A model of a single workshop for a new group. It is designed for a two-hour session, but suggestions for splitting it are also given. The aim is to establish cooperative work, in pairs and the group as a whole. The work explores ways of telling a story in pictures without the need for dialogue. Timings are given. They are approximate, but give a rough indication of how long should be spent on each activity. The major work in the session assumes three groups, giving ten minutes for discussion and planning, and ten minutes for each group to 'direct' the rest.

Physical warm-up	10 minutes
Walking round space crossing centre line, then naming the things in the room	10 minutes
In circle, throwing beanbag and giving name	5 minutes
Making random lines and shapes	10 minutes
Trust exercise (swaying)	10 minutes
Concentration game (dragon's treasure)	10 minutes
Pair work: *photographer and model*	10 minutes
Whole group: *photographic assignment*	40 minutes
Discussion of work done and final game	10 minutes

If only one hour is available, as is often the case when you are working in a school, the work can be divided into two sessions. The same theme runs through both, and thus continuity can be achieved with the building-up of experience.

first session	
Short physical warm-up	5 minutes
Beanbag and names	5 minutes
Lines and shapes	10 minutes

Trust exercise	10 minutes
Photographer and model	10/15 minutes
Discussion and game	10 minutes

second session

Short physical warm-up	5 minutes
Alternative trust exercises	5 minutes
Photographic assignment	40 minutes
Discussion and game	10 minutes

2.   A model of a four session course for a more experienced group. It is planned assuming two hour sessions, but can be adapted for shorter sessions, either by cutting or curtailing some of the preliminary work, or by extending over more than four sessions. Approximate timings are suggested. The aim of the work is to develop story telling skills, and explore how these can be used dramatically.

first session

Physical and vocal warm-up	15 minutes
Concentration game (e.g. *Salt and Pepper*)	10 minutes
Pair work: *Open the box*	10 minutes
A short devised improvisation, involving two objects taken from the box, to be shown to the rest of the group by each pair. It should be quite tightly controlled, lasting no more than two to three minutes	30/40 minutes
Commentary, working in pairs or threes. A brief discussion time to be spent as preparation, and then commentary and action performed.	20/30 minutes
Discussion of work done, briefing for next session and closing game	

second session

Physical and vocal warm-up	15 minutes
Trust exercises (e.g. talking through maze)	10 minutes
Just a Minute	15 minutes
Personal stories. They should have been briefed on this the previous session.	40 minutes
Interviews, to be done spontaneously, using about four people as interviewees, and encouraging 'questions from the floor'.	20 minutes
Discussion of work done, briefing for next session and closing game	

third session
Physical and vocal warm-up   10 minutes
Concentration exercise (e.g. *Matthew, Mark,*
   Luke and John)   10 minutes
Stories in a Circle, using traditional
  material, on which they should have been
  briefed the previous session   40 minutes
Break into small groups of three or four,
  and each group chooses one of the stories
  they have heard. Their task is to re-create it
  dramatically in a way which incorporates one
  or more storytellers to provide a narrative
  accompanying action. This work may well run
  over into the next session, depending on the
  size and nature of your group.   50/60 minutes
Discussion of work done, briefing for next
  session and closing game.

fourth session
Physical and vocal warm-up   10 minutes
Walking and naming objects in the room,
  staggering point and name   5 minutes
either complete the work begun in previous
  session *or* showing a friend round your room,
  choosing an object in each and devising short
  improvisation incorporating both   30/40 minutes
Dramatised narrative. Provide a synopsis of
  a story. The material can be drawn from any
  source, and can be based on suggestions
  elicited earlier from the group. It is not
  necessary for it to be traditional, nor
  conventional in any way. Ask them to identify
  the key episodes in the story and, in small
  groups, choose just one to work on. The aim
  is to present it dramatically in whatever style
  they wish, incorporating a storyteller. Each
  group's work should not last longer than
  two or three minutes, and they need to work
  quite fast to prepare it. The resulting work is
  run through, in sequence, and observed closely
  by chosen people to see how the episodes can be
  linked by further narrative, where necessary.
  The work is then performed again, this time
  with the narrators providing links between
  the episodes to make a coherent whole.   50 minutes

Closing discussion of work achieved and final game

Note: All the games and exercises mentioned above
are described fully in Chapters 1 – 3 of this book.

Short Script

The following is an example of the kind of short script which is useful
at many stages of your work. It can be used as a springboard for
improvisation, for work on character, or for different styles of playing.

A.   Are you going out again tonight?
B.   No. Why?
A.   I just wondered.
B.   Does it matter?
A.   No, of course not.
B.   Why did you ask, then?
A.   Oh, just making conversation.
B.   It's a very definite question. I mean – you could have
     have said 'has it stopped raining?' or 'what's on the
     telly?'. Why did you ask that question?
A.   Does it matter?
B.   No, of course not.
A.   Well, are you?
B.   What?
A.   Going out again tonight.
B.   What do you think?
A.   I don't know, that's why I asked.
B.   Does it matter?
A.   No, of course not.
B.   But it does, doesn't it? Otherwise why ask that particular
     question?

Productions

Funding a production
If you are mounting any kind of production, it will involve some
cost, however modest and economical your intentions. You do
need to make estimates before you start to ensure that you are not
left with a deficit and bills that cannot be met.

The list which follows has been compiled to cover all possible
areas of expenditure, and you can select from it those which are

appropriate. The costs against these headings are what you will have to cover, either from existing funds, ticket sales, fund-raising efforts, or grants from various bodies.

Professional fees, e.g. for director, musical director, choreographer, designer, technical director
Performance rights
Theatre licence
Purchase of texts
Travel expenses: to rehearsals
                  to venues (cast)
                  to venues (set and technicians)
Venue hire
Lighting hire
Additional lighting equipment (gels, bulbs and so on)
Sound equipment, hire or purchase
Set, construction materials
Costume, hire and/or materials
Properties, hire, purchase and/or materials
Printing: posters, tickets, programmes
Administrative costs, e.g. postage, telephone
Insurance

If you are working in a school, most of the 'expert' help you will be using is likely to be voluntary. However, the case with youth theatres may be different. You may well wish to engage the assistance of professional specialists, for the training which your members can experience from working with them. You are also less likely to have 'free' resources, such as lighting equipment.

It is common practice to scrounge materials, recycling materials rejected by local industries, hunting through jumble, and borrowing scaffolding, ladders and other bulky and expensive items. These are all worthwhile and healthy activities, but sometimes you will be forced to buy or hire expensive equipment, and one hire charge can wipe out an evening's takings, especially if you are touring your work to small venues. Transport costs can be especially crippling. You would be very lucky to cover your costs from door takings.

It is possible, however, to apply for financial assistance from a variety of sources. Town, district and county councils have budgetary headings under which the kind of work you are doing may well appear, and it is worthwhile finding out about these, to apply for grants either for specific events or an extended programme of work. Government agencies concerned with local development, both in urban and rural areas, can also be approached. Arts associations, regional and local, are often willing to give funds, especially towards professional fees.

It is worth cultivating all these agencies. If you make sure that they are aware of the work which your youth theatre is doing, and its value to the local community, you will find that they are likely to be willing to support it. For major projects, such as a large-scale production, or one which is to be toured to different venues within a community, you may need to apply to several bodies to ensure that you have sufficient funds to cover costs.

Thorough financial pre-planning, and the submission of realistic estimates of costs and project income, does a lot to assure funding agencies of the professionalism of your approach.

Performance venues

It is more likely that a youth theatre will consider taking a production to more than one venue than will a school group, though there is really no reason why this should be so. Either way, there is a great value in touring your work. It gives the young people involved the opportunity to play before audiences in which nobody knows them personally, and this gives them something of the experience which professional actors face all the time. Equally, it enables a wider public to see what they can achieve.

Whatever space you are playing in, for the time in which you inhabit it it becomes a theatre, and some spaces do so more easily than others. Every venue has its advantages and disadvantages, and you need to assess them before deciding to use it.

You have certain basic requirements, and need to ask some questions.

Playing space

Is it large enough to provide a playing area and room for the audience? Can it accommodate the set? What are the acoustics like? Are there any problems with exits and entrances for the actors? What is the maximum audience it can hold? Might it be too large to provide a good environment to play in:- this can sometimes apply to theatres, especially some of the older ones. If there are other areas in the building that are used, is anything else booked in for the date(s) you want it? If so, will it interfere with you in any way?

Technical and other resources

Has it a safe and adequate electricity supply? Are there sufficient electrical sockets for lighting and sound? What is the maximum electrical load the system will safely take? If it is equipped with stage lighting and you are not bringing in your own, is it well-maintained? Does it have a board which your lighting technician understands, and is it adequate for your purposes? If you are playing during daylight hours, can you blackout effectively? Are their sufficient chairs available to seat an audience? What and where are the toilet facilities? Is there someone who can prepare and provide refreshments, if you want to?

Backstage facilities

How much backstage space is there? Is there sufficient dressing-room space for your cast? Is there adequate lighting? Is there water available?

Access

Can you get the set in? What is the access like for the audience? Is there access for disabled people? Where is the nearest car park, 'bus stop, railway station?

Cost and income

What is the hire charge? Do you have to pay separate caretaking fees? Is there a local audience which is used to coming to this venue for entertainment? What is the maximum audience you can expect? What will they expect to pay for their tickets? Is there a local outlet for ticket sales? Are there other events happening locally which may clash with your dates and take away potential audience?

The perfect venue does not exist, but if you get satisfactory answers to most of your questions, you will have gone as far as can be expected to ensure that you are not choosing a totally inappropriate place to play.

Production Check list

This is a list of the things that need to be ticked off one by one during the final stages of the production process. Some items on it only apply to particular cases, for example, if the production is being toured, but many of them are applicable in most circumstances.

Cast, technicians and backstage staff

(a)   Dates and times of final rehearsals and performances to be

confirmed, checked, and distributed.
(b)   Deal with any problems with personal transport.
(c)   Estimate how many technicians and other personnel you need, and find the people to do these jobs.

Transport
(a)   Ensure that everyone can get to the venues, if you are touring. If necessary, arrange group transport.
(b)   Arrange transport for set, technical resources, and technicians/stage crew.

Technical, set and so on
(a)   Check the safety and efficiency of existing equipment. Hire any additional equipment needed.
(b)   Ensure that you have the right gels, and spare bulbs.
(c)   Check the lighting plot with the lighting technicians.
(d)   Keep a running check on the progress of set, costume, properties, and the colours and materials being used.
(e)   Arrange fire-proofing if necessary.

Licences (see below)
(a)   Performance licence and theatre licence(s) must be applied for at least four weeks before performance.
(b)   If you are selling any alcohol as refreshments – even glasses of wine – you need to apply for a licence for this too. Ask for advice from the local magistrates' court offices.

Printing and publicity
(a)   Posters, programmes and tickets to be designed and printed.
(b)   Outlets for ticket sales to be arranged.
(c)   Posters to be distributed.
(d)   Get a press release to your local paper, and arrange for a photograph, if possible.
(e)   Try to have the play reviewed if there is a reliable and intelligent critic on your local paper.
(f)   Complimentary tickets to be sent to anyone who has funded the production, and anyone you want to make friends with and influence.

Additional help at performances
(a)   Arrange a full team of front of house staff for every night, with one person managing.
(b)   Ensure you have enough people to sell and check tickets, sell programmes and refreshments.

(c)   Two people will be needed at every performance to act in emergencies. Nominate these, and ensure that they are provided with torches.

Venue(s)
(a)   Carry out a thorough check of capacity, safety, seating and so on.
(b)   Make friends with caretakers and key-holders.

Performing rights

Copyright exists on both plays and music for fifty years from the death of the writer or composer. If you are planning a production of a play which is still in copyright, you must obtain a performing rights licence by paying a royalty fee, whether you will have a paying audience or not. This applies wherever you are playing, in a school, community hall, or theatre – even in the street.

The royalty fee is based on the number of performances, whether the production is amateur or professional, and the anticipated size of audience. Once the fee has been paid, you receive a performance licence which gives you the right to stage the play in public within the limits of your stated intentions.

There are some contemporary works which have not yet been released for amateur production, and you will not be given permission to produce these.

To find out where to apply for the licence, look in the front pages of the text you are using, which will give the name and address of the agent or company which handles the copyright. The company which deals with the majority of performing rights licences in the UK is:

Samuel French Limited
52 Fitzroy Street
London W1P 6JR   telephone 071 387 9373

They are very helpful in dealing with general enquiries.

As far as music is concerned, the same general principle obtains, but there are a number of different categories, for instance whether the music is recorded or played live. The people to contact for advice are the theatre sections of the:

Performing Rights Society
29/33 Berners Street
London W1P 4AA   telephone 071 580 5544

The cost of the performance licence must be taken into account when you are budgeting a production. It is worth making enquiries about the cost when you are first considering using a particular play, and you should apply for the licence at least four weeks before the date of the first performance.

If you are producing an unpublished play, you should negotiate directly with the author for permission to stage it.

Theatre licences

If you are mounting a production in a licensed theatre, it will not be be necessary for you to obtain a theatre licence. However, theatre licences must be obtained if you are playing in any other building, such as a school hall, studio, or community venue. These licences are necessary for the safety of the public who will be your audiences, and are concerned with such matters as the electrical safety of the building, access, emergency exits and practice, and size of audience. These regulations apply just as much to school plays where there is a paying audience as to any other theatrical event.

A particular concern is the nature of the materials used in any set. If these are in any way a fire risk, they must be properly treated with a flame retardant. In general, wood and metal are 'safe' materials, but paper, cardboard, many plastics and cloth are all potentially hazardous. Naked flames are only allowed on stage in the most strictly controlled circumstances. This is so wherever you are playing, licensed theatre or elsewhere.

To obtain a theatre licence, apply in the first instance to your local council for advice on the right department to contact. This does vary between local authorities. If the building you are intending to use already has an entertainment licence, for functions such as wedding receptions, the additional licence for a theatrical event can usually be granted without too much trouble, as it will have been inspected regularly. Other venues can sometimes prove more difficult.

Licences are granted with the advice of the local fire officer responsible for the safety of public buildings. He may ask to inspect the set to judge its safety, and will test it for flammability if he has any doubts.

You need to give the dates you will be using the venue, and the licence will only be granted for those dates. It may well contain restrictions on the size of the audience, regulations covering gangways, tying seats together in rows, and specify a certain number of front of house staff.

Apply for licences well in advance, and if you have any doubts about the venues or the set you are using, it is worth talking frankly with the fire officer and taking advice. The fire officer does have the power to close down a performance if it is found that you are not complying with safety regulations.

Insurance

If you are running a youth group which is not covered by insurance by a parent body, it is worth considering whether you should get insurance cover for your general activities, as well as productions. Accidents can happen and losses can be incurred, and these can prove very expensive if claims for redress are made. The National Association of Youth Theatres (whose address is given below) operates a specially designed scheme for youth theatres in conjunction with an insurance company, and can advise you on this.

Contacts and help

The umbrella organisation for youth theatre in the UK is the National Association of Youth Theatres (NAYT). It offers a number of services to individual youth theatres and youth theatre practitioners, and its membership scheme gives free access to most of these. It publishes a bi-monthly magazine containing articles and information about all aspects of youth theatre.

Amongst its services are training for practitioners, a consulta-tionary script library and resource library (free loans to members), the publication of regional directories and resource packs. It can provide advice on funding, national and international links and exchanges, and operates an insurance scheme.

In Scotland, the Scottish National Association of Youth Theatres (SNAYT) offers advice, contacts and member services, and has close links with NAYT. The Drama Association of Wales (DAW), whilst being primarily concerned with adult amateur drama, offers resource hire to members, and has what is probably the largest script library in Europe, with facilities for both consultation and hiring. Another useful contact, mainly concerned with drama in education, is National Drama.

National Association of Youth Theatres
The Bond
180/182 Fazeley Street
Birmingham B5 5SE   telephone 021 766 8920

Scottish National Association of Youth Theatre
Old Atheneum Theatre
179 Buchanan Street
Glasgow G1 2JZ   telephone 041 332 5127

Drama Association of Wales
The Library
Singleton Road
Splott
Cardiff CF2 2ET   telephone 0222 452200

National Drama
Centre for the Performing Arts
College Street
Nottingham NG1 5AQ   telephone 0602 476202

Further reading

The following books may be available from French's Theatre Bookshop, 52 Fitzroy Street, London W1P 6JR (telephone: 071 387 9373).

General Stagecraft

Caught in the Act, video and leaflet; Youth Clubs UK, Publications Department, Keswick House, 30 Peacock Lane, Leicester LE1 5NY.

Fo, Dario, *Tricks of the Trade* (Methuen, 1991).

Gillette, A.S., *Stage Scenery: Its Construction and Rigging* (Harper & Row 1981).

Govier, Jacquie, *Create Your Own Stage Props* (A & C Black, 1989).

Griffiths, Trevor, M (ed.), *Stagecraft: the Complete Guide to Theatre Practice* (Phaidon Press, 1990).

Practice

Hake, Herbert, V., *Here's How: A Basic Stagecraft Book* (Samuel French, 1958).

Hogget, Chris, *Stage Crafts* (A & C Black, 1975).

Thurston, James, *The Theatre Props Handbook* (Betterway Publications, 1987).

Lentin, Louis, *Produce Your Play* (Ward River Press, 1982).

McCaffery, Michael, *Directing a Play. Vol 1* (Macmillan, 1991).

Miller, James, Hull, *Self-Supporting Scenery for Children's Theatre* (Meriwether, 1982).

Reid, Francis, *The Stage Lighting Handbook* (A & C Black, 4th ed., 1992).

Spolin, Viola, *Improvisation for Theatre: A Handbook of Teaching and Directing Techniques* (Pitman, 1974).

Stern, Lawrence, *Stage Management: A Guidebook of Practical Techniques* (Allyn & Bacon 1974).

Techniques

Thomas, Terry, *Create Your Own Stage Sets* (A & C Black, 1989).
Tomkins, Dorothy Lee, *Handbook for Theatrical Apprentices* (Samuel French, 1962).

Make-up for the stage

Baygan, Lee, *Make-up for the Theatre, Film and Telelvision* (A & C Black).
Basic Stage Make-up; a video produced by On Board publications (£36.37).

The Role of drama in education

Bolton, Gavin, *Towards a Theory of Drama in Education* (Longman).
Wagner, B. J., Dorothy Heathcote: *Drama as a Learning Medium* (Hutchinson).
Way, Brian, *Development through Drama* (Longman).

General Interest

Barker, Clive, *Theatre Games* (Methuen).
Berkoff, Steven, *I Am Hamlet* (Faber).
Brook, Peter, *The Empty Space* (Pelican).
Stanislavski, Constantin, *An Actor's Handbook* (Methuen)
Jodgson, J and Richard, E., *Improvisation* (Methuen)
Johnson, Keith *Impro* (Methuen).

Index